tw-eat more

a little book
with more big feelings
and short recipes
for very busy lives

@professor_dave

David K. Smith

Also by the author

*tw-eat – a little book with big feelings
and short recipes for very busy lives*

Published by David K. Smith

Printed by Amazon on Demand

ISBN 979-8-596160-60-4

Remembering Sam always
and with all my love to the 8yo

CONTENTS

TW-EATING MORE

Publishing *tw-eat*, the partner book to this, was one of my most fulfilling experiences. It tells the story of my family in a simple, honest way through the food we cook and enjoy – the love story between Sam & myself, the adoption of our wonderful, lively little boy, and Sam's untimely death leaving me as a single dad. I never thought so many people would be interested in our simple family recipes, the stories behind them, and the emotional resonance of what we eat. I want to thank everyone who read and enjoyed it from the bottom of my heart.

tw-eat

David K. Smith

Recipes and Reflections

"Such a beautiful book"

"Simple tweet length recipes"

"A story of love, loss and recovery"

"A love story to the two men in his life"

"A reminder of how food shapes memories"

"For those who cook and eat with love"

"Great recipes... simple but tasty"

"Heartfelt and simple recipes"

"Heartachingly beautiful"

Online Reader Reviews

Although this new book, *tw-eat more*, works perfectly as a stand-alone cookbook, it is also, most definitely, the partner volume to *tw-eat*. It completes the story of Sam and I, and finishes exploring the food that makes our family work. The cover was designed to match the first, with just a tweak to the colour of the logo. At our civil partnership, Sam's colour was blue and mine was purple. I conceived of these two books to be a symbolic matching pair in just the same way that Sam and I were.

After publishing *tw-eat*, family and friends got in touch to say: "What about this recipe?" or "Do you remember the time when...?" I also had many more recipes, and a rich treasure trove of memories, many of which I had held back from the first book – for example, our civil partnership and honeymoon never even got a mention! On top of that, daily life went on and I carried on testing and discovering new dishes. As the 7yo turned into an 8yo, he became increasingly interested in eating 'spicy' food, and so I began to explore global family cooking in which chillies played an increasing role. All of this convinced me that I needed to 'tw-eat' just one more time.

At the heart of the first book, surrounded by simple recipes, was an exploration of the central role of Sunday lunch in the food culture of our family. This is something I brought from my own childhood, and gifted to Sam, who helped weave it into the fabric of our family life. This book matches the format of the first, with simple recipes and  reflections organised in the same groupings but replaces the section on Sunday lunch with a central exploration of outdoor food and the barbecue. My own family has no real culture of outdoor eating, but for Sam's family it's a huge thing – this is something he gifted to me. Now, just like Sunday lunch, it has been woven into our family's food culture. We might only have a small back yard, with a bit of artificial grass, but as soon as the sun is out and the temperature rises above 18°C, we will be eating outside. I sometimes think that in our marriage, I brought the Sunday lunches while Sam brought the barbecues. I brought the comfort; he brought the sunshine.

Several people have asked me whether being a scientist was any influence on writing tw-eat. It is interesting to reflect that as scientists, we have years of training in writing accurate, but brief, experimental procedures, that can be replicated in laboratories anywhere in the world. In fact, this was the perfect training for creating simplified 'Twitter-style' recipes. Once again, in this book, the recipes are for two people unless stated otherwise, and oven temperatures are for a Fan oven (add 20°C for non-fan). In addition, synthetic chemistry is very like cooking in terms of the skills & techniques used in the lab. Indeed, if you want to see just how many chemists are passionate and talented cooks, just explore the Twitter hashtag #chemistswhocook.

One of the most amazing parts of publishing my first book, apart from the thrill of it being in print and holding a copy in my hand, was seeing people share what they have cooked from it – often copying me in *@professor_dave*, or using the hashtag *#TwEat*. As a scientist, I am used to people 'citing' my research papers, but seeing people cook themselves nourishing and enjoyable meals from instructions I have published is intensely satisfying. It has been fascinating to see which recipes people choose to cook, how they change things to suit their families, and what emotions the food evokes in them. At the heart of the *tw-eat* books is the deep interlinking between food and emotions. The ability of food to capture a transient moment, give solace and comfort in dark times, or create family memories, is remarkable. So often, families end up in the situation where food is simply fuel. With the recipes and reflections in *tw-eat*, I hope to show that food can be simple and fast to prepare, as demanded by family life, but can still be evocative, as well as delivering flavour and great comfort.

As in the first book, this is an honest description of what we actually eat. Everything has been tried and tested as part of family life. Once again, it is important to say that this is a collection – many recipes are lifted, adapted and modified from a variety of sources, which I try to acknowledge through the book. One of the biggest pleasures of publishing *tw-eat*, was when one of my food heroes, *Nigella* (I think we're on first name terms now) got in touch on Twitter to say she'd bought a copy! She's been an integral part of my kitchen for many years, it was a delight to think I am now a tiny part of hers.

Finally, I hope you enjoy this book and find some new family favourites. Many of the dishes are sufficiently simple that they are a perfect way to get kids (if you have them) started on cooking – the 8yo loves to help me out. I look forward to seeing what you choose to *#TwEat* about, and can only hope that some of the recipes and memories in here bring you as much comfort, flavour and enjoyment as they have brought us.

David Smith

SIMPLE SUPPERS – MEAT

CHICKEN YAKITORI

🐦 Glaze: 2tbsp *soy sauce*, 2tbsp *mirin*, 15g *caster sugar*, 1tbsp *sake* (or *dry sherry*). Heat & reduce until a bit thicker.

Thread cubed *chicken thigh* & *spring onion*, or *chicken liver* & *red pepper* on small skewers. Brush with glaze.

Grill/griddle until cooked, brushing glaze.

Serve with *lemon & mustard*.

👤 You must try this – the sweet, sticky glaze is a sure-fire winner, especially with kids. Cut the chicken small so it cooks quickly, these are dainty skewers not kebabs. You can skip chicken liver, and just make all the yakitori with thigh if you prefer. Personally, my favourite is yakitori *chicken gizzards* or *hearts*; I love the chewy texture, but it's too hard to find them in the UK!

There are not many photos of Sam and I together, because I am usually the photographer. I love this one, taken by my best friend from college and the best man at my wedding, Jonny, who lives and works in Japan. The photo was taken when we were with him at a kushiyaki restaurant. We had a fabulous night out enjoying all sorts of food on sticks with dipping sauces before heading on to party in a Tokyo rock bar!

SWEDISH MEATBALLS

🐦 Soak 50g *panko* in 75ml *milk*.

Soft-fry ½ fine-chopped *onion* in 10g *butter*. Add 1tsp *ground allspice*.

Mix 250g *minced beef*, 250g *minced pork*, ½ beaten *egg*, fried onion & soaked panko. Shape into meatballs.

Fry in *butter/oil* until brown, remove.

Heat 10g *butter*, ½ tbsp *flour*, stir, slowly add 200ml *chicken stock*. Add 100g *sour cream*. Add meatballs, cover, simmer 15 min.

Serve with *mash, lingonberry jam* & chopped *dill*.

👤 Meatballs remind me of our honeymoon, which we spent exploring Scandinavia, travelling right up the Norwegian coast into the Arctic Circle, and then back down through Sweden. We were lucky to enjoy a heatwave in Stockholm and just loved the handsome Swedish capital, its equally handsome men, its laid-back attitude and its meatballs. Of course, you can buy Swedish meatballs from *Ikea* – the 8yo loves them and they make a very quick tea, but these homemade meatballs, adapted from a *Diana Henry* recipe, are fab. You should, however, still get an *Ikea* jar of lingonberry jam – if you can't, just use cranberry sauce instead. This recipe makes enough meatballs for four, so you can freeze half of them after shaping them if there are just two of you.

CHICKEN, LEMON & BASIL TRAYBAKE

 Cut *potato* to 2cm dice.

Place in roasting tin with *chicken leg pieces* (bone in, skin on) and 2 squashed cloves *garlic*. Season with *salt & pepper* (especially chicken).

Toss in *olive oil*, squeeze half *lemon* over, throw squeezed lemon half in tin.

Roast, Fan 190, 30 min. Add *basil*, roast 10 min more.

Add 100ml *white wine*, reduce on hob.

Serve with roasting juices, *green salad* & more *basil* leaves.

A traybake – one of the easiest forms of cooking, yet utterly delicious. The 8yo loves it when I serve chicken on the bone, because he gets permission to eat using his fingers! This dish has all the flavour of roasted chicken, fragrant garlic, herbs & lemon, with chip-like potatoes, but only needs 40 minutes cooking time and 10 minutes of actual effort. Even better, using the splash of white wine to enhance the pan juices is the perfect excuse to open a cold bottle of your favourite tipple and make sure you have a very large glass of it with your dinner. It's perfect food for a summer afternoon in the garden.

ORECCHIETTE, BACON, COURGETTE & PECORINO

Cook 200g *orecchiette pasta*.

Fry 100g chopped *bacon*, 3 min.

Finely chop & add 1 small *courgette*, 1 *shallot*, 1 clove *garlic*, 5 min.

Add ca. 50ml *double cream*, heat.

Add cooked pasta, generously grate *pecorino cheese* over.

A simple, tasty pasta dish. Make the sauce while you cook the pasta, and you will have dinner on the table in 15 minutes. Obviously, Italians might use pancetta, but bacon is fine. For the pasta, you want something small and 'open'. Orecchiette are perfect and are one of my favourite pasta shapes for eating, but conchiglie or farfalle would work fine. In honesty, you can use whatever cheese you like - when checking my original tweet, I used Spanish *manchego*, and it was delicious (shhh – don't tell any Italians). However, for the purposes of the recipe, I have suggested a more conventional Italian cheese. If you haven't used *pecorino* before and always go for *parmesan*, it's worth giving it a try. As a sheep's cheese it has a cleaner, sharper taste, and goes particularly well with simple, light, vegetable-driven pasta sauces.

SHEPHERD's PIE

 Finely chop I *onion*, 1 *carrot*, 1 *celery* stick and gently fry in *olive oil*. Remove.

Brown 450g *lamb mince*, adding ½tsp *cinnamon*, *salt & pepper*.

Add 1tbsp *plain flour*, stir. Add veg, 275ml *vegetable stock*, 1tbsp *tomato puree* & 1tsp *thyme* leaves. Simmer, lid on, 30 min.

Put in baking dish. Top with loosely-riced *mashed potato*, drizzle with 25g melted *butter*, scatter 50g *cheddar*.

Bake, Fan 180, 25 min.

This Shepherd's Pie recipe is classic British family cooking comfort food. It's adapted from *Delia Smith*, but by keeping the mashed potato topping loosely riced and drizzling with butter, the top goes deliciously crisp as it bakes. The recipe is enough for four people – you can make half quantities, but rather like lasagne, it somehow doesn't feel right to make a small Shepherd's Pie. You can reheat leftover portions in the microwave. I might be crazy, but I think that (rather like a Lancashire Hotpot) Shepherd's Pie goes really well with *pickled red cabbage* – the acidity helps balance out the richness of the lamb, but you can always be more traditional and serve *peas*.

THAI-STYLE COCONUT LIME CHICKEN

🐦 Marinade 300g diced *chicken breast* in juice & zest of 1 *lime*.

Fry in 1tbsp *sunflower oil* & 1tsp *sesame oil*, 5 min.

Slice and add 1 *green chilli*, 2 *spring onions*, 15g *ginger*, 2 min.

Add 200ml *coconut milk*, 1tbsp *fish sauce*, 2 min.

Stir in chopped *coriander*, *basil*, *mint*.

Top with 2 *spring onions* cut in strips & more chopped *herbs*.

👤 I was going to call this a Thai Green Curry – it has most of the components and spirit of it. However, given the amount of 'stick' I got on Twitter for my preference for a tiny splash of cream in spaghetti carbonara, I thought I would just call it Thai-Style Coconut Lime Chicken so I didn't get accused of 'murdering' another classic! This dish is also great with less chicken and more veg – *baby sweetcorn* or halved *sugar snaps* are best. You can also replace the chicken with *mushrooms* and use *vegan fish sauce* to give a fragrant vegan dish. You don't need all three suggested herbs, you could just use coriander, but the combination is more 'Thai'. If you can get your hands on some *Thai basil*, then use that instead of the three herbs.

GAMMON and PINEAPPLE SALSA

 Cook *gammon steaks* on hot griddle, 3 min each side.

Mix ½ chopped *fresh pineapple*, ¼ chopped *red onion*, ½ chopped *red chilli*, juice of 1 *lime*, small handful chopped *coriander*.

Serve with *french fries* and possibly a *fried egg*.

Considering Sam lived all his life with cystic fibrosis and knew that ultimately his life would be limited by it, he had an incredible positive mental attitude. His ability to look to the future in an optimistic way was a massive influence on me, and is something I try to pass on to the 8yo. Sam very rarely got fed up, and if he did, it was usually about relatively trivial things, like frustration with me because I hadn't helped enough around the house. On the rare occasions Sam did feel genuinely low, gammon and pineapple was one of his go-to dinners. My contribution to his tradition was to persuade him to make a simple pineapple salsa to go with the gammon. The heat of the chillies and the acidity of the lime perk up the dish and help lift the lowest of spirits.

SLOW-ROAST SUMMER LAMB BELLY

Rub 3tbsp chopped *rosemary*, 2tbsp *yellow mustard seeds*, 1tbsp *garlic salt*, 2tbsp *celery seeds*, ½tbsp *thyme* leaves into 600g unrolled *lamb belly*, drizzle *olive oil*.

Roast wrapped in foil, Fan 150, 2 h, remove foil, Fan 180, 30 min.

Mix *asparagus* & sliced *red pepper*, *season*, drizzle *olive oil*, roast last 10-15 min.

Serve with thin mint relish (large handful chopped *mint*, ½ fine-chopped *shallot*, 2tsp *caster sugar*, juice ½ *lemon*, 1tbsp warm *water*)

You don't normally think of slow cooking as a summer activity, but in my opinion, this adapted slow-cooked lamb belly recipe from *Nigel Slater's* book *Eat* is surprisingly perfect for a sunny day. The secret to turning this dish into summer eating lies in how we usually serve it. I cut the lamb into strips that we eat with our fingers – dipping them into lemony mint relish along with roasted pepper slices and asparagus spears. If you need some carbs, then toasted flat bread (see page 99) also cut in strips is perfect, perhaps with some garlic butter. This is the way I loved to eat with Sam. We'd sit and chat about politics, life, friends and family – dipping, eating, and talking – with a nice big glass of wine, his eyes sparkling as he put the world to rights.

TOAD IN THE HOLE

 Toad

Mix 1 cup (130g) *flour*, ½tsp *mustard powder*, 2 *eggs*, 1 cup *water/milk* (120ml of each), *salt & white pepper*.

Remove meat from *good sausages*, shape in balls, fry in *sunflower oil*.

Heat *sunflower oil* in baking dish, Fan 210.

Add browned meatballs, pour in batter. Bake, Fan 210, 30 min.

Gravy

Fry *sliced onion* & 1tsp *sugar* in 20g *butter* until golden, add 1tbsp *flour*, slowly add 400ml *beef stock*, stir.

I know Toad in the Hole (or 'Frog in a Bog' as we affectionately call it in our house) is a classic that anyone in the UK can rustle up, but that is partly the point of this book – it's an honest depiction of what we actually eat. Also, the 8yo absolutely loves this and will definitely want the recipe when he's older! When I was a child, my Mum used to make Toad in the Hole with slices of *corned beef* instead of sausages (that's not necessarily a recommendation). Rather than using whole sausages, we like the *Nigella* approach of shaping sausage-meat into bite-size balls. I have given a recipe for how to lovingly hand-make onion gravy, but in honesty, I often just fry onions until golden and put them in *Bisto* gravy – so don't feel any pressure!

PORK, MUSHROOMS, GINGER, KIMCHI

Fry 200g sliced *pork steak* in hot *sunflower oil*, 2 min.

Add 15g sliced *ginger* & 200g quartered *mushrooms*, 2 min.

Add 1tbsp *soy sauce*, 1tbsp *mirin*, 100g *kimchi*, 1 min.

Add 1tbsp *rice vinegar* & 2 sliced *spring onions*.

Serve with steamed *Jasmine rice*.

This fusion of Chinese and Korean food is a super tasty, very fast stir-fry dish. The kimchi is the star here, lifting an average stir fry into something really special. I was unsure whether the 8yo would eat kimchi, but in fact, he loved the umami flavours and slight spice this dish delivers, and it was very quickly demolished. It would be easy to produce a flavour-packed vegan version of this dish by replacing the pork with *shiitake mushrooms*. I serve this with plain Jasmine rice. The 8yo adores plain rice, and since I got a rice cooker, which makes perfect rice every time with no effort, I have even found myself really enjoying its simple pleasures. However, this would also be great with *egg fried rice*, and I know some kids would prefer that. (In brief: Very quickly stir fry *egg* in *oil*. Add *steamed rice* that has been chilled in the fridge. Add 1tbsp *soy sauce*, *peas* and chopped *spring onions*. Fry till rice gets crisp fried bits).

SPAGHETTI al RAGU

Finely dice 1 *onion*, 1 *carrot*, 1 *celery stalk*. Gently fry in *olive oil*. Remove.

Fry 3 chopped rashers of *unsmoked streaky bacon* and 450g *minced beef* – as it browns, season with *salt, pepper* & 2tsp *dried Italian herbs*.

Add 1 glass *red wine*, reduce 50%.

Add cooked veg, *bay leaf*, 400g can *chopped tomatoes*, ½ can *water*.

Simmer 1-2 h, add water as needed. Serve through cooked *pasta*.

This photo shows the last physical meal Sam ever cooked for me. It was actually a few months after he died when I pulled this batch of 'Bolognese' sauce from the freezer – he had made it before he passed away. Just knowing food was so important to him, and that he had chopped, sweated, stirred, seasoned & tasted it, made for a very special, but sadly reflective moment.

The 8yo, like most kids, adores Spaghetti Bolognese, so there's almost always some of this in the freezer. I cook a batch for 4 people based on the recipe above and freeze the leftovers. Don't pile the sauce up on top of the pasta (it's supposed to coat it), don't use too much sauce, and don't ever ask for 'Spaghetti Bolognese' in Italy, it's not authentic – although they have something similar on *tagliatelle* or *pappardelle*.

PORK STEAK with DIY SAUCE

Bash *pork steaks*, coat in *seasoned flour*.

Fry in *butter/oil* (ca. 3 min per side), remove.

For cream sauce: Add 100ml *white wine*, reduce 50% scraping pan. Add 10g *butter*, 100ml *double cream*, pinch *salt*. Flavourings (choose from): *Dijon mustard, grain mustard, lemon* juice, *green peppercorns, tarragon, parsley.*

For lemon butter sauce: Add 100ml *white wine*, reduce 50% scraping pan. Add 25g *butter*, juice of half a *lemon*. Flavourings (choose from): *tarragon, parsley, sage, thyme, capers.*

This is really tasty and versatile, guaranteed to get your dinner on the table in 10 minutes. Once you have perfectly fried your pork steak, you then only need to decide what sauce you want to serve it with. The photograph shows a mustard & green peppercorn cream sauce, which is delicious, but as the recipe explains, you can easily select the sauce to make the dish suit your mood. Whatever you choose, the sauce will take up all the savour of the pork from the frying pan. To get it on the table, serve with deep-fried french fries (or bread), and some simple boiled vegetables (or side salad). With all the possible variation here, your family won't even notice you're essentially just cooking the same thing.

SLOW-COOKED LAMB & BLACK OLIVE TAGLIATELLLE

Gently fry 1 chopped *onion* in *butter* & *olive oil*.

Add chopped *garlic clove*, 350g *diced lamb shoulder*, 50g chopped *black olives*.

Add 100ml *white wine*, reduce 50%. Then add 250ml *chicken stock*.

Simmer 2 h, top with water (or Fan 140, 2-3 h, or slow cooker, 6 h).

Reduce. Add 200g cooked *tagliatelle*, finish with chopped *parsley*.

This is not a typical quick-cook pasta dish – but it doesn't take much work. Adapted from a *John Whaite* recipe, it delivers a massive smack of umami thanks to the black olives and qualifies as real comfort food. Ideally, put this in a slow cooker (or low oven) once you get to the 'long simmer'. You can then leave it with a lid on and head out for a long wintry walk. When you get back home into the warmth, all you need to do is boil some pasta and a super-satisfying supper is done. Me and the 8yo both love getting out in nature – honestly, these last few difficult years, it has helped to keep us both sane. This is just what I want to eat when we get home.

SIMPLE SUPPERS – FISH

S&M² (SAKE, MISO, SOY, MIRIN) MACKEREL

Marinade *mackerel fillets* in 2tbsp *sake* (or *dry sherry*), 2tbsp *miso paste*, 2tbsp *mirin*, 1tbsp *soy sauce*, 1tbsp *caster sugar*, 1 crushed *garlic clove*, 10g *grated ginger* for 1 h.

Grill fish under medium heat until just cooked, ca. 5 min.

Sprinkle with *sesame seeds* (optional). Serve with *rice & pickles*

The flavours of this dish take me back to Takayama, a rural Japanese town up in the mountains, famous for its sake, miso and beautifully preserved old town. We had a wonderful time exploring the traditional wooden buildings that line the streets, sampling different products – the photo shows Sam at a Sake brewery. This dish is healthy, very tasty and uses the classic Japanese combination that I refer to as S&M² (yes, I know). It needs to be served with pickles – I like *quick pickled cucumber* (see page 79), but a jar of *Japanese pickles* from an Asian supermarket would be easy and more authentic. Finish with *leaves* (dress with *olive oil, sesame oil & rice vinegar*) or *edamame beans*, and boiled *Japanese rice* sprinkled with a little *Shichimi Togarashi*. Although this is not one of her recipes, I very strongly recommend *Harumi Kurihara* for further simple approaches to Japanese flavour.

CLAM CHOWDER

Fine-dice & gently fry ½ *fennel*, ½ *onion*, ½ *leek*, 3 rashers *bacon*.

Add 150ml *white wine*, reduce 50%.

Add 1 litre *fish stock*, reduce by 25%.

In separate pan, melt 25g *butter*, add 20g *flour*, slowly add 100ml *milk*. Add this slowly to chowder to thicken.

Add *clams & sweetcorn* – if raw, give 5 min; if cooked, just heat.

Top with diced *tomato* & chopped *chives*.

Clam chowder is a must on the East Coast of America – a very special place for us. Sam was a 'West Wing' addict with a fascination for US politics & history. During Christmas 2007, he was very ill indeed in hospital. To cheer him up, I gifted him a trip to Boston, New York, Philadelphia and Washington DC. As soon as he had recovered, we made the trip and had an incredible time. In 2016, we made the same trip with the 8yo, also exploring some of rural Virginia and Pennsylvania. This clam chowder is not 'authentic', but it's absolutely delicious, and connects me with very happy memories.

BLOODY MARY PRAWN COCKTAIL

Chop ½ deseeded *cucumber*, small *avocado* & 1 *celery* stalk into dice. Add *cooked king prawns*.

Mix 150g *tomato passata* (or 150ml *tomato juice*), 1tbsp *Worcester sauce*, generous dash *tabasco*, good squeeze *lemon* juice, 1tbsp *vodka* (optional).

Mix all ingredients together and serve.

Sam loved a Bloody Mary – it was his brunch cocktail of choice on the morning after a 'long night'. One of my guilty pleasures is a proper 1970s prawn cocktail. So, this Bloody Mary Prawn Cocktail recipe is the perfect marriage between us. We often had this as a starter on special occasions – it's great for perking up the palate before a blow-out meal. Obviously, you can adapt the Bloody Mary sauce to your palate (and omit vodka for kids). To make a classic prawn cocktail instead: use shredded *lettuce*, chopped *cucumber*, juicy *prawns*, *cocktail sauce* (make your own using 1:1 *ketchup:mayo* with a good dash of *Worcester Sauce*), *smoked paprika* and *lemon* wedges.

SMOKED HADDOCK with CHIVE SAUCE

Place 2 *smoked haddock fillets* in frying pan, add 150ml *milk*.

Bring to boil, simmer uncovered 8-10 min. Remove fish.

Add 2-3tbsp *crème fraiche*, 15g *butter*, 1tbsp chopped *chives* & generous squeeze *lemon* juice. Heat until thickened, 2-3 min.

Serve with *mash & veg*.

This simple supper adapted from a classic *Delia Smith* recipe is very definitely the 8yo's 'happy place'. Ever since he was tiny, he has loved fish and cream sauce. It was something his Foster Mum used to cook for him before we adopted him, and I think that even still, it subconsciously makes him feel secure and contented.

If I'm being honest, I find making mashed potato a bit of a pain, but nothing else will do as an accompaniment here. The mash should be buttery, soft and indulgent, almost melting into the creamy chive sauce. Using the poaching liquor as the base for the sauce gives it loads of flavour and means you don't need to add any salt (but do check by tasting). Amusingly, one of my Twitter friends pointed out that in this case, on the plate, I appear to have created the British Isles, with the sauce as the Irish Sea. It's a bit worrying that Scotland appears to be missing – I love it north of the border and after all, it's where the smoked haddock came from!

MOROCCAN FISH and COUSCOUS

🐦 Mix 60g *flour*, 1tsp *paprika*, 1tsp *cumin*, ½tsp *cinnamon*, ½tsp *ground ginger*, 2 crushed *cloves*, *salt* & *pepper*.

Coat *haddock fillets* in spiced flour. Pan fry in *butter/oil*, 5-8 min.

Mix 100g *couscous*, 125ml *water*, 10g *butter*, *salt*, 5 min. Fluff up. Add chopped *dates*, *red pepper*, *parsley*, crushed *pistachios*.

👤 Underneath the aromatic, golden Moroccan-spiced crust is beautiful white flaking fish. It's paired with couscous which requires no more 'cooking' than pouring on hot water. It is important to load couscous with flavour & texture, or it can be dull. In this case, sweetness from dates (or *sultanas/dried apricots*), freshness from red pepper, herbal notes from parsley, and crunch from pistachios (or *toasted flaked almonds*). Serve with a wedge of *lemon*. If you want more heat, add ½tsp *cayenne pepper* to the spice mix, and scatter chopped *red chilli* over. You can replace the individual spices with ready-made *ras el hanout*. In Morocco, exploring Marrakesh's souk was a joy – every spice merchant makes their own unique *ras el hanout* mixed spice blend.

'BAKE-IN-THE-BAG' PRAWNS

 Wrap in foil: 200g *raw prawns*, 1 quartered *cob sweetcorn*, 1 sliced *courgette*, 1 thin-sliced *lime*, chopped *coriander*, 2tsp *paprika*, ½tsp *cumin*, 1tbsp *olive oil*, 25g *butter*, *salt & pepper*.

Place foil on baking tray, Fan 180, 15-20 min until prawns are pink & veg tender.

'Cook' *rice noodles*, place in bowl, spoon contents of package over.

One of the easiest things you will ever make – and once you've got the hang of it, you can change things around very easily. Basically, in your package along with the prawns you need (i) vegetables that will steam nicely in ca. 15 minutes in the oven (most tender veg will be fine with this treatment), (ii) something acidic, (iii) flavourings/salt and (iv) oil/butter. Swap the *lime* for *lemon* or *rice vinegar* to send this in Mediterranean or Asian directions. Change the *Mexican spices* for *Mediterranean-style herbs* or *soy sauce & ginger*. Choose vegetables to your taste (*asparagus, green beans, mange tout, mini sweetcorn, peppers, spring onions*). Essentially, you are building a ready meal and then letting the oven and foil package do the work for you. Serve with *pasta, tortillas* or *rice* instead of noodles.

GOAN FISH CURRY

Heat 1tsp *coriander seed*, 1tsp *cumin seed*, 3 *cloves*, 4 *black peppercorns* in dry pan. Bash in mortar. Add 1tsp *chilli powder*, ½tsp *turmeric*.

Heat 2tbsp *sunflower oil* in frying pan, fry ½ chopped *onion*, 5 min.

Add 1tsp *mustard seed*, chopped *garlic* clove & 15g *ginger*, 2 min.

Add spice mix from mortar, 1 min.

Add 1 fine-chopped *tomato*, 1 whole green *chilli* (optional), ½tbsp *white wine vinegar*, 25ml *water*, 3 min

Add 100ml *coconut milk*, 100ml *water*, ½tsp *sugar*, ½tsp *salt*, 2 min.

Add *white fish* cut in cubes, 3-5 min till just cooked. Shake don't stir!

Add 1tsp *white wine vinegar*, season, add chopped *coriander*.

I was tempted to put this in the *Saturday Indulgence* section because it looks complicated – but it's not! If you have all the ingredients ready at the start, it only takes 20 minutes and delivers the tastiest fish curry. I made this for Sam sometimes when he came home from hospital. He wanted something light, but packed with flavour, the kind of thing that couldn't come off a trolley in an NHS ward. This hit the spot totally. Serve with *cardamon rice*.

FISH PIE JACKET

Bake, cut in half, & hollow out 2 *jacket potatoes* (save the potato!).

Gently fry 1 sliced *leek* in *butter*. Add to 150g mixed *fish*, 100g *crème fraiche, parsley, chives*, ½tsp *Dijon mustard, salt & pepper*. Put in jackets.

Mix potato, 50g *cheddar*, 1tbsp *creme fraiche*. Top jackets.

Bake stood in muffin tray, Fan 180, 25 min.

Sam adored cooking a proper fish pie – it was one of his signature dishes – sadly I don't have his recipe any more. But in honesty, fish pie is a lot of effort to go to for supper, especially when it's just me and the 8yo. As soon as I saw this *John Whaite* recipe written down, I knew it was a sure-fire winner. It gives you all the fish pie 'love' in a simplified easy-to-eat format. For ease, you can use frozen 'fish pie mix' (cod, smoked fish, salmon) from the supermarket – I also like to throw in a few shrimp or prawns from the freezer. We eat it sat in front of one of our favourite things on the TV, like Dr Who, holding the slightly cooled jacket and scooping out the hot fish pie filling with a fork. It's just a perfect recipe!

PRAWN & PEA RISOTTO

 Finely chop and gently fry ½ *fennel* & ½ *onion* in *olive oil*. Do not colour. Add 1 sliced *garlic clove*.

Add 100ml *white wine*, reduce 50%.

Add 140g *Arborio risotto rice*.

Slowly add ca. 450ml hot *vegetable stock*, stir until rice is almost cooked.

Add 150g *raw prawns* & 2 handfuls *peas*, stir until prawns are pink, ca. 3 min.

Add squeeze *lemon*, shredded *basil*, *salt* & *pepper*.

This is one of my most-cooked recipes over the years. It's adapted from a *Jamie Oliver* idea, but adding fennel into the base, because it is just such a perfect match with prawns and is a good way of getting an extra portion of hidden veg into the 8yo! Often risotto is a soothing, comforting dish, but this one is bright, fresh and lively. It's one of the 8yo's favourite things to eat – clean bowl guaranteed every time.

CAJUN PRAWNS and RICE

🐦 Fry 1 clove chopped *garlic* in 1tbsp *olive oil* & 10g *butter*, 2 min.

Add 200g *raw prawns* & 2tsp *Cajun spice*, 2 min.

Add 150g chopped fresh *tomatoes* & 8 thick-sliced *spring onions*, 3 min.

Add *cooked long grain rice* (from 150g dry rice), season if needed.

Finish with handful chopped *parsley*.

👤 When we were a two-parent family, travel overseas to conferences and to meet collaborators was a key part of my job as a scientist. That has become much more challenging as a single dad. My final 'big solo trip' was to a conference in New Orleans – a city with an incredible food culture. This simple dish is inspired by my visit. For Cajun spices I use 'Joe's Stuff', which I bought while I was there. You can of course buy Cajun spice in a supermarket, or for fun make your own (blend: 3tsp *paprika*, 2tsp *garlic powder*, 2tsp *salt*, 1tsp *cayenne pepper*, 1tsp *onion powder*, 1tsp *black pepper*, 1tsp *onion powder*, 1tsp *dried oregano* & ½tsp *dried thyme*). Prawns are one of the 8yo's absolute favourite things to eat, so I often use them to introduce him to different flavours and tastes. It doesn't really matter what you do to them, he will still wolf them down, so it's a great trick for expanding his palate!

YUZU SCALLOPS, BACON CRUMB and MISO NOODLES

Marinade *scallops* in 1tbsp *soy sauce*, 1tbsp *mirin*, ½tbsp *yuzu juice*, 1tbsp *olive oil*, 5-10 min.

Grill 2 rashers *streaky bacon* to crisp - crumble.

Griddle *scallops*, 1-2 min per side.

Fry 3 sliced *spring onions*, 5g chopped *ginger* in a little *sesame oil*.

Add leftover marinade, 1tbsp *miso paste* & pre-cooked *udon noodles*, heat.

Serve with griddled scallops & crumbled bacon.

Yuzu is a great match for seafood, and when I found some fantastic scallops I was inspired to create this dish. Scallops are a luxury ingredient – pairing them up with noodles is a good way to stretch them into a main course. We had this as part of a 'Japanese Day' where I introduced the 8yo to the culture of Japan. We made maki together (see page 103), learned how to write our names in Japanese calligraphy, wrote a haiku, watched a Studio Ghibli movie, and ate this for dinner – perfect!

MEDITERRANEAN MONKFISH TRAYBAKE

In roasting tin, drizzle *olive oil* on halved *cherry tomatoes*, sliced *red pepper*, ¼ chopped *red chilli*.

Roast, Fan 180, 8 min.

Roll *monkfish fillets* in *lemon zest*, chopped *rosemary & salt*.

Fry monkfish in *butter* till golden, 3 min.

Add handful chopped *black olives*, *basil* & monkfish to roasting tin, Roast, 7 min.

Slice fish, serve with *parmentier potatoes*.

Monkfish is quite expensive, so this is a bit of a luxury supper, but it's so delicious – both fishy and meaty – and it stands up very well to strong Mediterranean flavours. In particular, black olives (perhaps surprisingly) pair perfectly with fish and form the umami backbone of this dish. Parmentier potatoes are described in more detail in *tw-eat*, but for ease of reference: cube *potatoes*, *season*, toss in *olive oil*. Roast, Fan 180, 30-40 min. This makes effective use of the oven – just start the potatoes 20 minutes before the vegetables go in. Sometimes, I invent and cook a dish that I really wish Sam was still here to taste and enjoy – this was one of those occasions.

SIMPLE SUPPERS – VEG

ASPARAGUS & GOAT CHEESE TART

Blanch ca. 12 *asparagus* spears in boiling water, 1-2 min.

Mix 100g *soft goats cheese*, 50g *cream cheese*, 1tsp *thyme* leaves.

Cut *puff pastry sheet* to fit asparagus (with a border).

Spread cheese mix on pastry leaving border. Arrange asparagus on top.

Brush border with beaten *egg*.

Bake, Fan 180, 25-30 min.

This is a perfect dish for kids to prepare, as most of the work is in the preparation of the tart – like baking but without an unhealthy sugar-filled product (much as I love such things from time to time)! The 8yo loved making it, and as a massive fan of asparagus, he enjoyed eating it too. It's a perfect Spring tart when asparagus is in season at the local shops. It is best served with a mixed dressed salad, ideally including some fragrant herbs. Obviously, the basic idea is versatile, for example, it would work very well with sliced *mixed peppers* (no need to blanch) instead of the asparagus.

CAVOLO NERO & HAZELNUT PAPPARDELLE

Cook ca. 200g *pappardelle*.

Cut 300g *cavolo nero* in ribbons and boil, 5 min, drain well.

Fry 1 chopped *garlic* clove in *olive oil*, add cooked cavolo nero.

Add cooked pasta.

Finish with handful *toasted hazelnuts*, chopped *flat leaf parsley*, 2tbsp *olive oil* & grated *pecorino*.

I grow cavolo nero on the allotment with the 8yo. In honesty, I think the slugs probably get as many of the leaves as we do, but we have great fun collecting a handful each time we go to the allotment during the Autumn and deciding what to do with them. This was one of our favourite outcomes. If your cavolo nero has tough 'ribs' in it, cut those out when you slice it. This tasty vegetarian pasta is a version of a *Diana Henry* dish from her must-buy book *Simple*. She adds red chilli and a little orange zest with the garlic, so do feel free, but I found this version was more 8yo-friendly and tasted just as good. She also uses parmesan cheese, but I like the sharp nuttiness of pecorino. It's easy to omit the cheese or replace it to make a vegan version of the dish. This is a great Autumn/Winter pasta recipe – it's the crunch of the hazelnuts and the rich bitterness of the cavolo nero that make it a bit special.

GREEN CHILLI & MANGO CHANA DHAL

Add 125g *yellow chana lentils*, 100g fresh *chopped tomatoes*, ¼tsp *turmeric* to pan. Add 500ml *water*. Bring to boil. Simmer 30 min.

In 1tbsp *sunflower oil*, fry 1tsp *cumin seeds*, 1 chopped *green chilli*, 150g 1cm-diced *mango*, 3 min (until mango starts to soften).

Add cooked lentils, stir.

Add 1tsp *salt*, ½tsp *sugar*, squeeze of *lemon juice*, chopped *coriander*.

We eat vegetarian food one or two days a week, and increasingly, I am trying to incorporate a vegan meal. I'm not an instinctive vegan cook, so I need to hunt round for inspiration. This recipe came from *Nisha Katona*'s beautiful book *The Spice Tree*, which although not Vegan, has some great ideas. I have made this on summer evenings – usually after a long, hot, stressful day. The refreshing sweet-sour flavours revive me, and the fruity mango puts a smile back on my face.

I have been to India with work a couple of times and find the vibrant cities fascinating. Dhal was a key part of one of my most unique food experiences, when I visited the spectacular Golden Temple in Amritsar. Part of Sikh culture is to feed people for free in their temples. Join the line, and you become one of the thousands of people every day fed a simple but tasty dhal, sitting on the floor in long rows. Once you're finished, you take your plate with you and help with the washing up. A memorable experience in a beautiful place.

CHIPOTLE HALLOUMI WRAP

 Cut 160g *halloumi* in 1-2cm cubes.

Fry halloumi in *sunflower oil* until golden with 1 rough chopped *yellow pepper*, ½ rough chopped *red onion* & 1tsp *chipotle chilli flakes*.

Make salsa (fine-chop *tomato, red onion, coriander, green chilli, lime*).

Place halloumi mix on warm *tortilla*, add salsa, finish with *sour cream*.

Such a tasty vegetarian dish – honestly, I struggled to photograph it before we ate it. Wraps are great family food. Everything sits in bowls on the table, and people just take as much of all the different things as they want. This is one of the 8yo's favourite ways of eating – it avoids stress at the table. If you are cooking for chilli-sensitive kids, then leave the chilli flakes out of the halloumi/veg mix and dial down the chilli in the salsa (see below). You can put a bottle of *chipotle hot sauce* on the table. In fact, I might even prefer it that way. Making a homemade fresh & lively *pico de gallo salsa* is a useful skill – you can match the ratios of ingredients to your family's palate. As a starting point, for 2 people try: 2 *tomatoes*, ¼ *red onion*, ½ *green chilli*, handful *coriander*, good squeeze *lime*. I think it's better to very finely hand-chop everything with a good knife – if you use a food processor, it turns to mush and, in my opinion, loses its freshness and character.

MUSHROOM RISOTTO with PARMESAN CRISP

Fry fine-chopped small *onion* in *olive oil* & *butter* till soft.

Add 200g sliced *mushrooms*, fry.

Add 150g *Arborio risotto rice* & 50ml *white wine*, stir, reduce 50%.

Slowly add ca. 500ml *vegetable stock*, stirring.

For parmesan crisps, put small piles of grated *parmesan* on lined baking tray, Fan 180, 5-8 min.

Finish risotto with knob *butter*, handful grated *parmesan* & *black pepper*.

Risotto is just the most comforting thing to make and eat. The constant stirring is a kind of reflective kitchen therapy for the soul and the soft textures and gentle autumnal flavours here are deeply soothing. If you want to tweak this recipe slightly, add some thick chopped *Italian salami* – it's great, but then it doesn't really fit in the vegetarian section. Parmesan crisps are not an essential addition, but they do make the risotto feel a little bit more special. The 8yo loves them and they effectively cook themselves while you do all that stirring and reflect on how your life could have been different.

COURGETTE & FETA FRITTERS

🐦 Grate 500g *courgettes*, sprinkle with *salt*, stand in sieve, 30 min. Gently squeeze, drain.

Mix with 3tbsp *flour*, 1 beaten *egg*, 100g crumbled *feta*, 3 fine-chopped *spring onions* & handful chopped *dill* (or *mint*).

Shape into 6 fritters.

Fry till golden in *oil/butter*. Turn once carefully – fragile.

👤 Without doubt, courgettes are one of the most depressing vegetables you can grow on an allotment. Delicious when small and sweet, turn your back on the plant for just a week or two, and suddenly they balloon into gigantic marrow-sized monstrosities. Not only that, but one plant can produce such prodigious quantities of courgette, that I sometimes think a few fields of them could solve world hunger. The real problem though, is that although you end up with enormous quantities, they are just not the most inspiring thing to eat. I'm therefore always on the look-out for good courgette recipes - this is adapted from a *Nigel Slater* recipe, and is one of my favourites. These fritters are great with salad, crusty bread, and a good quality spiced chutney.

GLAZED BEETROOT & APPLE with CELERIAC MASH

🐦 Boil 2 *potatoes* cut in 3cm chunks, 5 min. Add ½ *celeriac* cut in 3cm chunks, 8-10 min.

Drain, dry, mash, dry, season, add 20g butter.

Melt 25g *light brown sugar*, add 25 ml *balsamic vinegar*.

Add 1 sliced *apple* and 3 roasted *beetroot* cut in wedges. Glaze, 3 min.

Finish with toasted *hazelnuts*.

👤 The first time I took Sam out for dinner in York, way back in 2006, I knew that given his love of good food, it had to be somewhere special. One of the most unique places in York was *Vanilla Black*, a tiny innovative restaurant cooking high-end vegetarian food. Sam was not initially impressed by the idea of a vegetarian restaurant, but we had a fabulous meal there, and in the process, I convinced him that I knew a thing or two about food! We were simultaneously disappointed and delighted when Vanilla Black closed in York but moved on to great acclaim in London. This dish is adapted from a recipe in the Vanilla Black cookbook. In honesty, it is somewhere between 'simple supper' and 'Saturday indulgence'. If you roast the beetroot yourself (peel 3 small *beetroots*, drizzle with *olive oil*, wrap tightly in foil, roast, Fan 180, 50 min) it's probably weekend cooking, but if you use pre-cooked beetroot, it's a simple supper in 20 minutes.

CHEESE & ONION CAULIFLOWER

🐦 In roasting tin, put *cauliflower* cut into florets, *onion* cut in wedges, a sprig of *thyme*, 2tbsp *olive oil*, *salt* & *pepper*.

Roast, Fan 180, 25 min. Toss.

Add grated *gruyere* (be generous). Roast, Fan 180, 5-10 min.

Serve.

👤 Don't tell the 8yo – because it's a family rule that we never talk about food in a negative way – but I really don't like boiled cauliflower. The crumbly texture with a slightly slimy exterior just repels me. However, roasted, it is a completely different vegetable – the heat and dryness of the oven encourages it to take on a nutty flavour, and the texture improves dramatically. Combining roasted cauliflower with the sweetness of roasted onions in this cheat's version of cauliflower cheese makes for a ridiculously tasty and simple dish. This is a staple in our house. It's just perfect with leftover roast meat, and becomes the star of the plate – an unusual situation in which the meat is actually just the side dish. However, it would also be great on its own, or with a green salad and is one of the simplest, tastiest vegetarian suppers you will ever make.

VEGETABLE TEMPURA with SOY GINGER DIP

Dipping sauce: 2tbsp *soy sauce*, 2tbsp *mirin*, 2tbsp *rice vinegar*, 1tbsp *fish sauce* (optional), 5g grated ginger.

Batter: 60g *plain flour*, 60g *corn flour*, 150ml ice cold *fizzy water*. Mix very lightly with chopsticks – don't worry about a few lumps.

Dip *vegetables* (e.g. sliced *pepper*, sliced *mushrooms*, whole *asparagus*) in batter, deep fry in *oil* (180°C) until crisp & pale gold.

Drain on kitchen roll, serve immediately.

One of the most evocative places I ever went with Sam was Mount Koya in Japan. It is the religious centre of the Shingon Buddhists, who adhere to a strict Shojin Ryori vegan diet. We stayed the night in a monastery, which was an incredible and tranquil experience. We were served a beautiful dinner, including the most perfect tofu, and show-stopping vegetable tempura. The following morning we got up early for a Buddhist prayer service, then walked in the mist and fog through the atmospheric Okunoin cemetery to the Hall of Lanterns, where two lanterns, one donated by an Emperor, one by a peasant woman, have been kept burning continuously for almost 1000 years. The resonant living culture, food, and unique atmosphere will stay with me forever.

CRUNCHY PANEER & SPINACH CURRY

Chop & fry 2 small *onions*. After 5 min add 2 chopped cloves *garlic* & 15g grated *ginger*. Continue until onions are golden.

Add 1tsp *ground cumin*, 1tsp *ground coriander*, 1tsp *turmeric*, 1tsp *salt*, 1 min.

Add 400g *can tomatoes* & 1 whole *green chilli*, 20-30 min.

Cut ca. 200g *paneer* into cubes, toss in 3tbsp *semolina* & 1tsp *garam masala*. Fry in *sunflower oil* until golden, 5 min.

Add 250g *baby spinach* to curry, 2 min.

Add crunchy paneer, squeeze of *lemon* juice, *black pepper*. Serve.

This is a fantastic, simple, curry and was one of Sam's favourite dishes to eat and cook. I love paneer curries too and always choose to eating them when visiting India. The crunchy coating for the paneer here is a clever *Hairy Bikers* idea, and adds texture to the dish, something that's sometimes missing in vegetarian food. This curry is guaranteed to convert the most reluctant carnivore to vegetarian food, and is perfect with naans or flatbreads.

SPAGHETTI 'RIANIMARE'

Cook 150g *spaghetti* in salted water.

Chop large handful *black olives*, the rind of ½ small *preserved lemon*, ½ *red chilli*, handful *parsley*.

Stir chopped ingredients into cooked pasta with a good glug *olive oil*.

Christmas 2020! On the 23rd December my 'Covid tracker app' sent me a notification to say we had to isolate until the New Year. Our modest Christmas plans got written off and the two of us hunkered down in the kitchen. At least the shopping was done, and we had lots to sustain us. Once self-isolation was complete, the 8yo went off to spend a day with his Nanny & Grandad – our support bubble. As I collapsed at my kitchen table and looked at the bombsite of a house after 8 days of enforced Christmas house arrest, I just wanted to eat something reviving after all the excess of Christmas food. This bowl of pasta completely hit the mark. It combines salty, sour, hot and fragrant, with these four key components delivering a big flavour punch. Even better, this requires no cooking other than boiling a pan of spaghetti. In the recipe, I suggest 75g pasta per person, a good size for a light lunch – use 100g each for a dinner sized portion, but it's not really a dinner pasta. I have called it spaghetti 'rianimare' – before the purists complain, this is not a 'real' Italian dish, but I did feel truly 'revived', so I think the name is wholly appropriate.

A QUICK TEA

CRAB & PEA PASTA

Cook 175g *pasta* (I used *trofie*)

Fry 1 sliced *garlic* clove in 25g *butter* until soft.

Add 150g *crab meat*, 150g *frozen peas* & a good squeeze of *lemon*. Heat until peas are defrosted.

Add 2tbsp *double cream*, season with *salt* & generous *black pepper*, stir through cooked pasta.

The Yorkshire Coast is one of the 8yo's favourite places – he once told me: "Daddy, it makes me happy in my heart when we go to the beach". As soon as we get to the beach, he pulls off his shoes and socks, and just runs for the sea with a massive grin on his face. It's a shame we don't live closer to Cornwall – I'm sure he'd grow up to be a surfer dude! I sometimes cook this pasta dish if we bring home a dressed crab. More often, however, I use one of the pots of crabmeat you can buy in most supermarkets. Like all the best pasta dishes, it is very simple and only takes as long to put together as the pasta takes to cook. As the 8yo gets a little bit older, this is exactly the kind of thing I could imagine him cooking by himself, especially if he is feeling a bit sad, and wants to use a simple supermarket ingredient to transport him to his happy place at the seaside.

CRUMPET RAREBIT

🐦 Gently soften ½ sliced *leek* in butter, 5-10 min. Do not colour.

Add 2tsp *flour*, 150ml *double cream*, 75g grated good *red cheese*, 1tsp *Dijon mustard.*

Grill 3-4 *crumpets* on bottom side.

Top with cheesy mix. Grill until golden.

👤 OK, so it's not really a rarebit, but the use of leeks is kind-of Welsh. Putting it on a crumpet makes for the perfect hand-held cheesy, creamy, oozy snack. It really does need a crunchy salad on the side to help cut through the richness though. This adapted *Nigel Slater* recipe can itself, easily be adapted further – replace the leeks with onions for a cheese and onion version. More radically, replace the red cheese with a soft blue cheese and the leek with apple. Or just go 'full rarebit', get rid of the cream, replacing it with a little less beer and a splash of Worcester sauce. Basically, it's easy, it's cheesy, and more importantly, when you feed it to the 8yo, he happily sits on the sofa and eats it while watching Netflix. Simple teas like that are worth their weight in gold.

FISH FINGER TACOS

Cook 6-8 *fish fingers* according to pack instructions. Cut into 4.

Mix 1 chopped *avocado*, 3 chopped small *vine tomatoes*, ¼ fine-chopped *red onion*, ½ chopped *jalapeno chilli*, juice of ½ *lime*, small handful chopped *coriander*.

Mix 3tbsp *sour cream*, 1tbsp *mayo*, 1tbsp *sriracha*, juice of ½ *lime*.

I guarantee that kids will love these fish finger wraps, and it mixes things up a bit from the usual fish fingers, chips & beans. You can tailor the chilli content to taste – it's easy to hold back on the chillies and then add extra chillies to a separate adult portion. This is one of those meals where we put bowls on the table and help ourselves to whatever we want – interactive eating. To make the wraps close to being proper tacos, buy mini wraps, or cut larger wraps into smaller circles. They become proper hand-held morsels – the 8yo always manages to surprise me with just how many he can eat! This is a perfect tea for the end of the week – other than chopping, mixing and putting some fish fingers in the oven, it's no effort for loads of flavour and lots of fun.

GRILLED CHEESE and 'STUFF'

 Butter two slices *white bread.*

Make an 'inside-out' sandwich with filling (*grated cheese + stuff*) on the unbuttered side and buttered side facing outwards.

In dry frying pan, fry sandwich (ca. 2-3 min per side) until golden, press occasionally with fish slice.

If you do this already, you will think: "Why on earth did he put this in a cookbook? I want my money back!" But if you don't already do this, it will change your life! Sam introduced me to this super-quick lunch/tea, and is now something that I probably eat more than anything else. A bit like cheese on toast, but no need to get down on your knees and peer under the grill to see if it's done, and a meltier, softer easy-to-eat finish. A toastie without the mess of the toasted sandwich maker. It's endlessly versatile. Simple fillings would be *just cheese, cheese & ham, cheese & pickle, cheese & chutney,* even *cheese & tuna mayo,* but really your imagination can take you wherever you want. Got leftover *pico de gallo salsa* from Mexican night, put it with *cheese* for a spicy sandwich. Take fried *onions, mango chutney,* chopped *red chillies, coriander,* a pinch of *garam masala & cheese,* and you get a heavenly Indian-style sandwich. Grilled perfection.

BUBBLE & SQUEAK

Chop/mash leftover *roast potatoes, parsnips & veg.* (Add a little extra *mashed potato* – only if needed)

Mix in just enough beaten *egg* to bind. Season with *salt & pepper.*

Fry in a disc 1-2cm deep until golden, ca. 5 min, flip halfway.

Serve with leftover *roast meat & sauce.*

Roast dinner leftovers are a great way of getting a quick Monday night tea on the table after that difficult first day of the week at work. The 8yo loves Bubble & Squeak, and often asks for it on Mondays – so it's not even like leftovers are unwelcome! Bubble & Squeak is a British classic, but often badly made, with mountains of mashed potato blanketing all the flavour. You *can* bulk this version out with extra mash, but it's better not to have to bother making mash – it also tastes better without. If you know you want Bubble & Squeak, cater Sunday lunch generously. Using leftover roast potatoes & parsnips gives depth of flavour. The leftover Sunday lunch veg are also added (throw in *frozen peas* if you are short). Bubble & Squeak is particularly good with pork & apple sauce, duck & cherry sauce, or beef & horseradish sauce – again, all leftovers. For more in-depth information on Sunday Roast cooking see the dedicated chapter in *tw-eat.*

ROASTED PEPPERS & BURRATA

Slice 2 *red peppers*.

Roast in *olive oil* with 1 crushed clove *garlic*, 1tsp *thyme leaves*, *salt & pepper*, Fan 180, 15 min.

Add 8 halved *cherry tomatoes* & ½ sliced *red chilli*, 15 min.

Serve with *burrata* & lots of *crusty bread*.

A delicious, simple, light tea, with fabulous colour and contrasting flavours and textures, that will make you feel like you're on holiday even if you're stuck in your own kitchen for the hundredth day of a Covid lockdown. If you want to smarten it up a bit and avoid the pepper skins, then first cut the peppers in half, grill them to blacken the skins, allow to cool, peel off the skins and then slice the peppers. You can then mix the sliced peppers with all the other ingredients in the roasting tin and simply roast for 15 minutes.

This dish sparked a good discussion with the 8yo, which illustrates perfectly how we think and talk about food. He wasn't completely sure about the wet texture of the burrata, although he tried it and said it was 'ok'. He told me he would prefer the slightly firmer texture of *mozzarella* (which would also be fantastic in this dish – so it's a good call and illustrates that he has a great palate). Anyway, now I know, I can save some money on his portion and keep all the delicious, cool, milky, oozing, expensive burrata for myself.

OGGY's POT NOODLE HACK

Take lid off *Pot Noodle*, add *boiling water* to mark.

Also pour boiling water over small *frozen veg* (e.g. *peas, sweetcorn, chopped mixed veg*).

After 4 min, drain veg using sieve, add to Pot Noodle, stir, add sauce.

Deep breath – it's confession time! Sometimes, when I'm in a hurry, I give the 8yo a Pot Noodle. In Japan, where Instant Noodles are an acceptable part of life, this behaviour would be viewed as normal. However, in the UK, this is considered by some as the very worst in parenting, bordering on abuse. Certainly, when I shared this fact on Twitter, it evoked a strong response as you can see – although strong responses can, of course, be par for the course on Twitter. In some ways I agree, I don't really *want* to feed the 8yo Pot Noodles, but sometimes, needs must. Anyway, to save my blushes, Mark Ogden, a friend who many years ago I worked alongside in the lab in Oxford, shared this brilliant hack with me - Pot Noodle with extra veggies, so you can feed your kids in 4 minutes and feel less guilty. What did the 8yo think? 'Mmmmm, thank you Daddy, that was actual tasty'.

Replying to @professor_dave
There are so many more healthy and nutritional things one can prep in 10mins. Wonderful example of today's lamentable parenting.
9:53 · 23 Jan 20 · Twitter for iPhone

BACON-WRAPPED HALLOUMI

Cut 160g *halloumi* into 'fingers', wrap each finger in a rasher of *streaky bacon*.

Fry in *sunflower oil* until golden.

Pour boiling water onto 200g *frozen peas*, drain. Add to 50g *watercress* and 4 sliced *spring onions*.

Dress greens: 1tbsp *olive oil*, 1tbsp *cider vinegar*, ½tsp *grain mustard*.

When I mentioned on Twitter, I had published *tw-eat*, this was the first dish one of my friends wanted to read in the book. Having forgotten to put it in first time round, and with it being one of my best family dishes, I knew that by popular demand, it simply had to appear in *tw-eat more*. The fresh sweet peas and bitter watercress are a delicious combination that both kids and adults will enjoy. If your kids really won't eat the watercress, does it matter? Just let them leave it. You can always replace it with some milder leaves like *lamb's lettuce* – but I do think the pepperiness of watercress is an integral part of the dish against the saltiness of halloumi and bacon.

1-2-3 PANCAKES

🐦 Put <u>1</u>00g flour in bowl. Add <u>2</u> eggs. Mix. Slowly add <u>3</u>00ml milk, whisking. Add pinch salt. Leave 30 min. (Makes 8)

Get *sunflower oil* very hot in frying pan – ladle in thin layer of batter, tilt pan to spread. Leave 1 min till golden. Shake to loosen. Toss.

Serve topped with whatever you want or keep warm in low oven.

👤 In this house, pancakes usually only happen on Shrove Tuesday. Every time, I think how tasty and easy they are, then forget all about them again. By putting them in the book, I will hopefully remember to cook them more often. The method is as easy as 1-2-3 (flour, eggs, milk). For toppings, I like leftover *roast chicken, mushrooms, spring onions, cheese & BBQ sauce,* but *cheese & fried mushrooms* are great. Or why not go crazy with leftover *lamb & mint sauce* or reheated *curry*? On Shrove Tuesday, sweet pancakes with *lemon & sugar* are practically the law. The recipe makes 8 full-size pancakes. In one way, it feeds 4. But if you want savoury & sweet pancakes, it feeds 2. If your child is the 8yo, it feeds him. If you want the respect of your kids, you must toss pancakes properly, by flipping in the air. As you can see, it's never too soon to practice (even if it is with a cold pan)!

OMELETTE

Beat 2 *eggs* with *salt & pepper* (and ca. 25ml *milk*, optional).

Get *butter* hot in frying pan – pour in egg, pull back edges of omelette as they set, tilt pan allowing liquid to run into gap.

Add toppings – e.g. grated *cheese*, fried *mushrooms* etc.

Heat, gently loosen from pan (use spatula if needed), cook until golden

Slide out of pan, allow to fall onto plate folded in half.

Serve with crunchy *salad*, *bread & butter*.

I know that an omelette recipe is superfluous for anyone who has ever been in a kitchen, but the emotional significance of this dish is such that it should be in the book. This is what me and the 8yo both eat, sat on the sofa wrapped in a blanket, if we have been poorly. The pure comfort of egg and cheese is what we crave. Omelette (and scrambled eggs) have played this role for me ever since I was little. I stretch my eggs for both dishes with a little milk – probably because that's what my Mum always did – but it does also make the final texture softer and more soothing. The act of love in trying to produce a golden omelette that turns out of the pan perfectly for the 8yo when he has been feeling poorly says more than any number of words can.

SATURDAY INDULGENCES

WAFFLES

Dry: 150g *SR flour*, 1tbsp *cornflour*, 1tbsp *caster sugar*, ½tsp *salt*.

Wet: 240ml warm *milk*, 25g melted *butter*, 1 *egg yolk*, 1tsp *vanilla extract*.

Slowly add wet mix into dry mix, combine.

Whisk 1 *egg white* & 1tbsp *caster sugar*. Gently fold into batter.

Leave to stand as long as you can, 10-30 min. Cook on hot waffle iron, ca. 3 min, Serve with *bacon* or *fruit* and *maple syrup*.

Waffles were what the 8yo would eat every Saturday at *The Pig & Pastry*, before lockdowns curbed his habit. Adorably, when he was 6, he once told me that he had "adopted Little Ted from the charity shop, and what adopted children need is waffles and lots of hugs". The hunt for a good Saturday morning waffle recipe has been a challenging mission. Separating the egg into yolk and white, whipping the white and folding it in, although being a bit of a pain, gives the lighter waffle I was searching for. This much batter will fill a standard waffle iron and make four 12cm square waffles. If you want more, double the quantities of batter (you can freeze cooked waffles and reheat them in a toaster). If you want your waffles to look 'Instagram-pretty' with ragged edges, rather than being ugly square blocks, don't completely fill the waffle iron – you avoid the mess of spilling waffle batter, and get nice rustic edges, like on the photograph.

APPLE & CINNAMON PANCAKES with ICE BERRIES

Dry: 125g *plain flour*, 1tbsp *sugar*, 1tsp *baking powder*, ½tsp *salt*, ½tsp *ground cinnamon*.

Wet: 115g *milk*, 1 beaten *egg*, 25g melted *butter*.

Mix wet into dry, add 1-2 peeled, cored, grated *eating apples*.

Fry in melted butter pan with *sunflower oil*. Flip when 'holes' appear & bottom golden.

Serve with handful of half-defrosted *berries & maple syrup*.

We have a lot of love for Saturday morning blueberry pancakes and bacon in this house (see the recipe in *tw-eat*). This apple & cinnamon version is a delicious way of re-inventing that recipe. The pancakes are great with bacon, or with raspberries or blackberries, but I think they are particularly good with 'ice berries'. What do I mean? Basically, I mean you get some berries out of the freezer, and then because it's early in the morning, you don't really have time or energy to defrost them properly so you put them in a sieve and pour a little hot water through them just to take the edge off. You end up with cold berries that are soft on the edges and still a little frozen in the middle – call them 'ice berries' and it almost sounds like you made some effort. I told the 8yo they were half berry, half ice lolly. They go perfectly with the warm, fragrant apple pancakes. A great way to start the weekend.

BOILED EGG & MARMITE SOLDIERS

 Toast 2 slices of *bread* per person, *butter*, spread thinly with *marmite*. Cut crusts off bread then cut into soldiers

Cook large *eggs* (1 or 2 per person) in water at rolling boil, 5 min.

Serve and get dipping!

As I wrote about in *tw-eat* when describing the recipe for *Pop's Pasta*, Sam adored marmite. When he was really ill, the powerful flavour it delivered from just a small amount on toast was one of the few things he could face eating. This is a simple weekend breakfast legacy to him that is simultaneously the best way of eating marmite and the finest way of eating boiled eggs you will ever find. The salty yeasty punch of marmite and the simple rich indulgence of a perfectly boiled egg with a soft yolk are ideally matched. Of course marmite is... well... a marmite ingredient, but if you're one of those who love it, then once you've tried this you'll find your knife hovering over the marmite jar every time you boil an egg.

CHICKEN KATSU CURRY

 Katsu Sauce

Rough chop 1 *onion*, gently fry in *oil* till golden, 10-15 min.
Add 1 clove sliced *garlic,* 10g chopped *ginger*, 5 min.
Add ½tbsp *Madras curry powder*, ¼tsp *turmeric*, ¼tsp *ground star anise*, *black pepper*, 2 min.
Add 10g *plain flour*, stir. Slowly add 250ml *chicken stock*, stirring.
Add 1tsp *tomato puree*, simmer 5 min.
Blend until smooth. Reheat when needed.

 Chicken

Bash two *chicken breasts* or *fillets* until flattened.
Dip in *seasoned flour*, then beaten *egg* then *panko breadcrumbs*.
Fry in 50-100ml *sunflower oil* in pan until golden (ca. 5 min each side).

Truly the gateway meal for getting kids to love curry. Katsu Curry is mild, tasty and the crispy chicken is a sure-fire winner. Ever since he was very small, the 8yo has loved it – look at that 2yo hand in the photo – he couldn't wait to eat it! Serve the sauce on the side and kids can dip the sliced crispy chicken into it as much (or as little) as they want. Something acidic on the side is nice – Japanese pickles from a jar are ideal. Although the sauce takes a little time, it can be made in advance and reheated when needed, so getting dinner on the table is very fast. You can always scale up the sauce and freeze some. Serve with simple steamed rice with a sprinkle of *Shichimi Togarashi*.

CHIPOTLE CHILLI CON CARNE

Chop 4 rashers *streaky bacon*. Fry in casserole, set aside.

Season 400g diced *beef shin* (stewing steak) with *salt* & *pepper*, brown in casserole, remove.

Fry 1 diced *onion*, 5 min.

Add ½ diced *red pepper*, 1 sliced *garlic* clove, 5 min.

Add 1tsp *cumin*, 1tsp *unsweetened cocoa powder*, 1 min.

Add beef, 1-2tsp *chipotle chilli flakes*, 400g can *chopped tomatoes*, ½ can water, 1 *bay leaf*, bring to boil.

Lid on, Fan 140, 2.5 h.

Add 1 drained can *red kidney beans* & fried bacon, 30 min.

A luxury Mexican-style chilli for a winter Saturday – perfect after a long cold walk. You can always replace the 2.5 h in the oven with a day in the slow cooker if you want a really long walk! In Mexico, chilli is often made with diced rather than minced meat. Shin of beef gives the tenderest, chunkiest chilli you will ever taste. I am cooking for the 8yo, so I hold back a bit on the chilli, if you want more, then add chopped red chillies with the cumin. The quantities here are enough for 2-3 hungry people – I get some leftovers for a jacket potato the following day. Serve it up with *rice, sour cream* and extra *red chillies.*

PRETZEL ROLLS

 Preparing (makes 6)

Mix 450g *plain flour*, 5g *dried yeast*, 1½tsp *salt*, 2tsp *sugar*, 40g melted *butter*, 260ml water.

Knead to smooth dough. Prove, covered, in oiled bowl, 1 h.

Knock back, shape into six 125g rolls on lined baking sheet.

Cover, leave to rise, 30 min.

 Baking

Boil ⅓-filled large pan of water. Carefully add 50g bicarbonate of soda (it fizzes). Poach buns, 30 sec on each side. With a slotted spoon, lift buns back onto lined baking sheet.

Brush with beaten *egg*, sprinkle *sea salt*, with sharp knife gently mark 'X' (or other shape) on top.

Bake, Fan 200, ca. 25 min.

Sam adored pretzels. I think it was partly a salt thing – cystic fibrosis patients have an imbalance in salt levels and can crave salty food as a result. He loved these pretzel rolls – satisfying to bake, and surprisingly easy for a spectacular finish. The bicarbonate boil gives them their gorgeous colour. Speaking chemically, it raises the pH and means the Maillard reaction (which causes things to brown on baking) works super-fast! The recipe is adapted from *Carol Hilker*'s book *Dirty Food*. These awesome rolls are as good with a bowl of soup or stew as they are stuffed full of pulled pork or slow-cooked brisket. Make them!

PULLED PORK

🐦 Mix 2tsp *smoked paprika*, 2tsp *cumin*, 2tsp *black pepper*, 2tsp *brown sugar*, 1tsp *salt*. Rub into ca. 1kg *pork shoulder*.

Put 1 sliced *onion* & 1 *sage leaf*, in slow cooker, place pork on top, add 150ml *India Pale Ale* & 50ml *cider vinegar*.

Slow cook, 6 h (or in casserole, Fan 130, 4 h, add *water* if needed).

Remove pork, 'pull' into shreds with two forks.

Skim fat off liquid, strain, add 3tbsp to 150ml *good barbecue sauce*.

Mix sauce through pork.

👤 So easy, so tasty – put everything in a slow cooker, leave it for the day and come back to delicious pulled pork. I have suggested using a medium pork shoulder, which will generously serve 4-6, but would serve 2 with *lots* of leftovers! You can scale the recipe easily – just use less/more rub & sauce. This pairs perfectly with Pretzel Rolls (page 63) & Homemade Slaw (page 65). If you put all three together, it's a lot of effort, but makes for a lovely cooking-filled Saturday and a great sense of satisfaction. You can buy good barbecue sauce, but if you are going for it, you should make your own (170g *ketchup*, 25g *black treacle*, 25g *golden syrup*, 60ml *cider vinegar*, 60ml water, ½tsp *salt*, ½tsp *black pepper*).

HOMEMADE SLAW

🐦 Very finely slice ½ *small white cabbage*, 1 *carrot*, ¼ *red onion*.

Add 2tbsp *mayo*, 2tbsp *sour cream*, 1-2tbsp *cider vinegar*, 1tsp *sugar*, 1tsp *celery seed*, ½tsp salt, pinch *garlic powder* & *black pepper*.

Mix. Leave to stand in fridge, 30 min.

👤 I love slaw! It's exactly what I want on the side of pulled pork, fried chicken, burgers, or in fact any of the home-cooked 'junk food' you can find in these books. The crunchiness and acidity combine to cut through the Saturday indulgence and at least help you feel you've got a few vegetables inside you, even if they might be coated in mayo & sour cream. Sam and I always used to argue about slaw – he said the vegetables should be cut ultra-thin with a mandolin, while I preferred to use my Japanese chef's knife, which gives a slightly thicker slaw. Looking back, I wonder why we wasted all those words, but equally, arguments like that are a vital part of the fabric of married life.

For variation, *fennel, red cabbage, beansprouts* or *apple* are excellent additions or replacements. The *celery seed* can be replaced with other fragrant flavourings like *caraway seed*, chopped *rosemary* or *sesame seed*. A dash of *mustard* or *wasabi* can lift the slaw. Finally, swapping the vinegar to *white wine vinegar* makes a sharper slaw, while *rice vinegar* (and 1tsp *soy sauce*) can send it in an Asian direction.

SLOW-COOKED TEXAS-STYLE BRISKET

Mix 1tbsp *chilli powder*, 1tbsp *salt*, 2tsp *black pepper*, 2tsp *brown sugar*, 1tsp *garlic powder*, 1tsp *mustard powder*, 1tsp *cayenne pepper*, ½tsp *dried oregano*, 1 crushed *bay leaf*, rub into 1kg *beef brisket*.

Roast, Fan 160, 30 min.

Add 250ml beef stock, then water to 1.5cm depth in tin. Cover in foil.

Roast turning twice, Fan 130, 2-3 h (until fork tender).

Slice and serve with the roasting juices.

This recipe gives a lovely spiced crust on the brisket – you then carve it into thin slices and serve with some of the roasting juices. It's great in a hot sandwich, but also nice with American-style veggies like roasted sweet potatoes, pumpkins, sweetcorn or peppers. This general approach to cooking brisket is versatile – you can change the rub to North African spices or Mediterranean herbs. You can also throw in some veggies that survive casserole-style cooking with the beef when you wrap it in foil, giving a whole meal in one parcel. Like pulled pork, this is great cooking for a crowd (1kg brisket will serve 4-6) – make Pretzel rolls, slow roast the meat, make slaw, and all dig in while you play board games. Sam was the one who organised our social life – he was the extrovert; I am the introvert. In honesty, I miss throwing parties like that but as a single dad, it's just so hard to have the energy.

MEATBALLS and BROAD BEANS

 Meatballs

Mix 250g *beef mince*, 50g *panko*, fine-chopped small *onion & garlic clove*, 1tbsp each chopped *parsley, mint & dill*, 1tsp chopped *capers*, 1tsp *cumin*, ½tsp *coriander*, ½tsp grated *nutmeg*, ½tsp salt, pinch each *cinnamon, ground clove, allspice & pepper*.
Add ½ beaten egg, shape into meatballs.
Fry in olive oil until brown, Remove.

 Beans and Assembly

Blanch 250g *broad beans*, 2 min. Drain, cool, remove skins from half.
Put 2tbsp *olive oil* in meatball pan, fry 3 sprigs *thyme*, 2 sliced *garlic cloves*, 5 sliced *spring onions*, 3 min.
Add skin-on beans, 1tbsp *lemon juice*, 50ml *chicken stock*, 10 min.
Add meatballs, 300ml *stock*, cover, simmer 25 min.
Add *extra herbs*, squeeze *lemon juice*, skin-off broad beans, serve.

 Kids love meatballs but are less convinced by broad beans. We grow them on our allotment, and the 8yo loves to pick and pod them, which is half the battle won! This (believe-it-or-not) simplified *Ottolenghi* recipe serves 2. It's a fragrantly herbal way to eat meatballs and a tasty way to use a broad bean glut – serve it with *rice* or *flat-breads*. It gives your spice cupboard a workout, but it's not hard. Half the beans are removed from their inner skin to reveal the bright green jewel-like heart. This looks good and gives two different textures.

'CHINESE' DUCK with POTATO PANCAKES

 Duck

Prick skin of *whole duck*, rub with 2tsp crushed *Szechuan peppercorns* & generous *salt*.

Roast on wire rack in tray, Fan 180, 25min. Pour off fat.

Then roast, Fan 100, 75 min. Pour off most of fat.

Pour 125g *runny honey* over duck.

Roast, Fan 160, 15 min, baste with pan juices. On final baste, add 75ml *soy sauce*.

Remove, rest, serve with pan juices.

 Pancakes

Mix 250g cold dry *mashed potato*, 75g *flour*, 1tsp *baking powder*.

Whisk 125ml *milk* & 2 *eggs*. Add to potato mix. Stir

Fry spoonfuls of batter in *sunflower oil* until golden brown, 2-3 min per side. Keep warm in oven.

This adapted *Tom Kerridge* recipe is lovely weekend cooking and makes a great alternative to a roast dinner. It does take some effort (hidden in the wording is the fact you must make dry mashed potatoes in order to make the pancakes), but it is utterly delicious. This is great with peas or braised lettuce, I like to combine the two and serve it with Petits Pois a la Française (see *tw-eat,* p. 86). This is the kind of thing I cooked for Sam on special occasions.

HAM HOCK and SAVOY CABBAGE

 Ham hock

Coat *ham hock* (ca. 600g) in *olive oil*, roast, Fan 160, 30 min.

Gently fry 1 rough-chopped *onion*, 1 thick-sliced *carrot*, 1 sliced *celery stick* and 1 smashed *garlic* clove in *olive oil*.

Add 100ml *white wine*, reduce 50%.

Add 1litre *chicken stock* and ham hock, simmer 1.5-2 h until tender.

 Dressing, Cabbage, Finishing

Mix 4tbsp *olive oil*, 1tbsp *lemon juice*, 1tbsp *red wine vinegar*, 1tsp *Dijon mustard*, *salt & pepper*.

Cut *savoy cabbage* in ribbons, blanch in salted boiling water, 4 min, drain.

Take chunks of meat off ham hock, add to cabbage in pan, add dressing and 50ml *ham cooking water*. Stir, warm, serve.

 This is a delicious, relaxing, slow Saturday afternoon cook. It is adapted and significantly simplified from a *Spuntino* recipe to ensure the ingredient list is manageable in tweet form without losing the heart of the dish. The soft meat, vibrant cabbage and sharp dressing are a fabulous combination. It just needs serving with plenty of crusty bread to mop up the juices.

BEER CAN CHICKEN and HOMEMADE BBQ SAUCE

 Chicken

Open *tall can American beer*, drink 150ml.

Mix 2tsp *paprika*, 2tsp *light brown sugar*, 2tsp *salt*, 1tsp *celery salt*, 1tsp *dried oregano*, 1tsp *mustard powder*, 1tsp *black pepper*, 1tsp *ground cumin*, 1tsp *garlic powder*, 1tsp *chilli powder*.

Rub *large chicken* with 2-3tbsp of dry rub.

Place 2 sprigs *rosemary* in beer can, place chicken onto can so it is standing up. Stand in roasting tin.

Roast, Fan 200, ca. 1 h, until cooked (or cook on large BBQ with a lid).

 BBQ Sauce

Gently fry ¼ chopped *onion* & 1 chopped clove *garlic* in 1tbsp *sunflower oil*.

Add 100g *ketchup*, 100ml *cider vinegar*, 1tbsp *American mustard*, 1tbsp *light brown sugar*, 1tsp *Worcester sauce*, simmer 10 min.

This is a fun, flavoursome way to cook chicken. It's a *Paula Deen* classic Southern States US cooking Any recipe that starts with drinking beer is a sure-fire winner! It can be barbecued, I almost put it in the next section – but you do need a big barbecue! The chicken roasts from the outside and steams with the beer from the inside, giving delicious crunchy skin and soft yielding flesh. To serve, add salads, sides and good homemade BBQ sauce. The dry rub quantities are enough for two chickens – it will keep in an airtight container.

BARBECUES

THE MAGIC OF BARBECUE

 There is nothing better than a hot sunny day, with a fine spread of food laid out on a table in the garden, or in our case, back yard. My own family doesn't have a tradition of barbecuing. Other than camping trips, I don't recall ever cooking outdoors with my parents. However, for Sam's family, the barbecue is a 'big deal'. The gathering of the whole family for an outdoor feast is a fixture of summer weekends. The 8yo will play with his cousins, Sam's dad will bustle round the barbecue, and his mum will produce incredible side dishes from the kitchen. The table groans with food, everyone talks over the top of everybody else, drinks are poured, stories & jokes are shared, and it's just the most fun. Having grown up with this, Sam was passionate about the importance of outdoor cooking & eating, and it was something I was delighted to incorporate into our own family life.

This section illustrates our family approach to the barbecue. It contains some classic meat & fish dishes, as well as vegetarian options and some stand-out side dishes. The secret of a good barbecue is to have a few things on the table that really make it special – as you will see, these can be very easy to put together, but with minimal effort, they elevate the whole experience to the next level, moving it far beyond shop-bought burgers & sausages and a bagged salad.

In terms of barbecue cooking, it is vital to let the initial blast of heat die down, otherwise you just cremate everything. Wait until the coals are coated in white ash and the flames have gone. Another good tip is to load your coals asymmetrically in the barbecue – this gives a hot side, and a cooler side. This means you can move food to the cooler side once it is cooked, or if the coals get a bit feisty. Of course, you can do far fancier things with indirect heat on barbecues, and with smokers, but all the recipes here can be cooked on a typical simple family barbecue. If the weather fails you, then they can just be cooked on a hot griddle pan in the kitchen instead.

PROFESSOR DAVE's BARBECUE BURGER

🐦 Mix 250g *minced beef* (10%+ fat), ¼ fine-diced small *red onion*, handful *panko*, 1tsp *ground coriander*, ½tsp *ground cumin*, salt, *pepper*.

Add ½ *beaten egg*. Shape into patties, chill.

Barbecue (or griddle), add slice *cheese* & cover with a lid for last 2 min.

Serve in *brioche bun* with fried sliced *mushrooms & BBQ sauce*.

👤 It's essential to have a good burger recipe for the perfect barbecue and I've spent a lot of time on this one. I love these burgers with a hint of spice – it enhances the flavour but does not dominate. You can leave out the cumin & coriander for a great, more traditional burger. The recipe makes 2 very large burgers, 3 medium burgers or 4 child-sized burgers. The secrets are: (i) to avoid the burgers being dry, don't use 'extra lean' minced beef; (ii) add panko breadcrumbs, they hold onto the fat and stop the burger drying out; (iii) don't add too much egg, just enough to bind. If you are going to the effort of homemade burgers, you must serve them on a very good brioche burger bun (supermarkets sell them but there is also a recipe in *tweat*). For barbecue sauce, I really like *Red's Kansas City Style*, but you will find your own favourite, or you can use the recipe on page 70.

HALLOUMI BURGER with BEETROOT DRESSING

 Slice block *halloumi* into two thin slices, trim to size of roll.

Peel & grate 1 large *beetroot*. Mix with 100g *natural yoghurt*, 1tbsp *white wine vinegar*, 6 chopped *mint* leaves, *salt & pepper*.

Barbecue/griddle halloumi 3-4 min per side, turning 90° for pattern.

Put in *brioche bun*, top with beetroot relish.

Why shouldn't vegetarians have delicious burgers to eat. I'm not a massive fan of vegetarian dishes that pretend to be meat – I understand why vegetarians like them, but as someone who eats meat, I can never really see the point. If I'm having vegetarian food, I want it to be unique – making the very most of its non-meat origins. This is an adapted *Nigel Slater* recipe that is one of our favourites. In honesty, I have changed just one thing. He makes this burger with feta, but I struggled to griddle it effectively – the moisture content is just too high. I replaced the feta with halloumi and this tasty burger was born. *Nigel*'s beetroot relish is delicious – I didn't change a thing about that. Just like any burger, you should serve this up on a good quality brioche roll. It's always a nice touch to grill the open faces of the roll to give it a bit of colour and texture.

HAKE, LEMON and HERBS

 Place 2 *hake fillets* on kitchen foil.

On one fillet, place thin *lemon* slices, very thin *fennel* slices, chopped herbs (e.g. *parsley, dill*) *salt, pepper & olive oil* (or *butter*).

Place second fillet on top of first, flesh sides together, wrap tightly in foil. Leave to marinade, 30 min.

Barbecue foil parcel 5-10 min (depends on size of fish & heat of grill).

This dish was prepared by Sam at his very last family barbecue and was a genuine showstopper. He bought the spectacular hake you see in the photograph from Leeds City Markets to feed about ten people as the centrepiece of a barbecue feast at his parents' house. Sam loved nothing more than cooking for family, and I like to think you can see the love he had for his family in the photo!

You can easily do something similar with more ordinary-sized fish fillets. All the flavour gets packed into the fish within the parcel. This is a great general approach for cooking any fragile fish on a barbecue – for example, salmon is fantastic barbecued in a parcel with soy sauce, mirin, lime juice, ginger and spring onions. The parcel locks in the flavour, prevents the fish from sticking to the grill, protects it from the direct heat, and makes for easy serving. If it rains, cook the parcels at Fan 180 for 10-20 min.

WATERMELON and HALLOUMI

🐦 Mix 2 cubed large wedges *watermelon*, 150g halved *cherry tomatoes*, 2 *spring onions*, small handful *coriander*, ½ *red chilli* (optional) & 1tbsp *olive oil*. Chill

Rub *ciabatta* slices with *olive oil*, barbecue/griddle.

Slice block *halloumi* in two thin slices, barbecue/griddle.

Load grilled ciabatta with melon salsa, top with halloumi.

👤 This is a *Nigel Slater* recipe and is one of the most delicious things you will ever eat on a hot summer afternoon. The cool crisp salad, the chewy grilled ciabatta, the salty warm barbecued halloumi – it's perfect and simply could not be improved. Our little back yard catches the afternoon and evening sun. I made this for the 8yo (who was 5 or 6 at the time) one glorious afternoon. I was enjoying a glass or two of chilled white wine, he was in and out of the paddling pool, which makes the whole thing less relaxed than it probably sounds! Watermelon is possibly the 8yo's very favourite thing to eat, so this dish is his idea of summer heaven.

CHICKEN TIKKA KEBABS

Mix 1 crushed *garlic* clove, 1tbsp *tikka spice mix*, 1tbsp lemon juice & 1tbsp olive oil in 100ml *natural yoghurt*.

Cube 4 boneless *chicken thighs* and marinade in yoghurt mix for 1 h.

Thread onto skewers with slices of *red pepper* (*onion* is also good).

Barbecue until chicken is cooked, 5-10 min.

Serve with *mint/yoghurt* dressing, *Indian chutneys*, *salads* and *flatbreads*.

Kebabs are a great option on the barbecue – kids love them, and you can tailor what you put on them to the specific tastes of your family. I prefer to use chicken thighs to chicken breast as they have a higher fat content, which means they are less likely to dry out. They also (in my opinion) have much better flavour. It's worth buying metal skewers that you can re-use, but when you turn them, remember they get very hot!

BLACKBERRY & APPLE SALAD

Salad: ¼ *red cabbage* & ¼ *red onion* both finely sliced, 75g *baby spinach leaves* sliced, 1 small *apple* cut into matchsticks, 100g *blackberries*, 20g toasted *hazelnuts*, 1tsp toasted *caraway seeds*.

Dressing: 4tbsp *olive oil*, 2tbsp *cider vinegar*, 1tbsp *maple syrup*, 1tsp *Dijon mustard*.

Mix and serve.

So often, all of the attention at barbecues is focussed on what's on the grill – the quality of the meat, and the spices, the marinades, the sauces. However, one of the best ways of making your barbecue extra special is to have a signature salad on the table and then just barbecue something simple, but high quality, as an accompaniment. This fantastic barbecue salad, adapted from a *Diana Henry* recipe, is perfect for this approach. It relies on the classic late summer combination of blackberry & apple, placing them on a slaw-style base. It's crunchy, tasty and with all that fruit and a maple mustard dressing is pretty much guaranteed to encourage kids to enjoy salad too – the 8yo completely demolished it! Once you've put your 'effort' into making this unique salad, all you need to do is serve it with some simply barbecued top-quality butcher's sausages & crusty bread. You are pretty much guaranteed a barbecue to remember, and you will be relaxed enough to enjoy a drink and a chat with friends and family.

SIMPLE BARBECUE SIDE SALADS

 Tomato Salad

Slice good quality *tomatoes*, arrange on small plate.

Sprinkle ½tsp *caster sugar*, pinch of *salt*.

Add finely chopped ¼ *red onion* and small handful *capers*.

Drizzle 1tbsp *olive oil*.

 Quick Pickled Cucumber

Cut ½ deseeded *cucumber* into half-moons.

Soak in 25ml *white wine vinegar*, 25ml *water* & 1tbsp *caster sugar*, 30 min.

Drain & serve.

 Watermelon Salad.

Cut *watermelon* into cubes.

Toss with handful chopped *mint*.

Dress (optional) with: 1tbsp *olive oil*, 1tbsp *lemon* juice, 1tsp *caster sugar*, ½tsp grated *ginger* (optional).

Celeriac Remoulade

Chop ½ small *celeriac* into finest matchsticks possible.
Dress with 3tbsp *mayo*, 1tbsp *lemon juice*, 1tsp *Dijon mustard*, ½tsp *caster sugar, salt & pepper*.
Leave to stand in fridge, 30 min.

 Beetroot, Sour Cream & Horseradish.

Cut 2-3 *cooked beetroot* into cubes.
Mix 2tbsp *sour cream* with 1tsp *horseradish sauce*.
Stir beetroot into cream sauce.

 Caprese Salad.

Slice 2-3 good quality *tomatoes*. Season with *salt & pepper*.
Tear ½ *mozzarella* into chunks scatter over.
Add small *basil* leaves.
Drizzle 1tbsp *olive oil*.

Every barbecue needs a salad, but sometimes it's tempting to do little more than reach for a bag of salad or chop up some lettuce & cucumber and put out a bottle of salad cream. The ideas given above are not elaborate, but they are fast and tasty and will bring something different and colourful to your barbecue table. I think that certain salads marry well with certain dishes. For example, barbecued oily fish, like mackerel, just cries out for a tomato salad, or something acidic like pickled cucumber. Smoked fish, sausages or gammon are a perfect match with celeriac remoulade. Barbecued steaks are moved to the next level with beetroot, sour cream and horseradish. Experiment with these salads and find out what your flavour preferences are. Try to marry up flavours to make your individual barbecue dishes come together on the plate into a delicious meal, using just one or two well-chosen simple salads to make your barbecue more special.

ALLOTMENT SALAD

Slice 2 *courgettes*, brush with *olive oil*, barbecue/griddle.

Boil podded *broad beans*, 3 min. Cool. Remove bright green hearts from outer skin.

Mix courgettes, beans, *watercress*, crumbled *feta*, chopped *mint*.

Dress with 2tbsp *olive oil*, 1tbsp *lemon* juice, 1tsp *grain mustard*, *salt & pepper*.

A simple salad made with courgettes & broad beans brought home from the allotment and eaten in the garden. We had this with an over-chilled glass of white wine when Sam had been on a bread-making course, and I had been working on the allotment. For full disclosure, I must confess that I would struggle to get the 8yo to eat this. He'd prefer it if I replaced the feta with *mozzarella*, swapped the bitter watercress for sweeter *lamb's lettuce* and maybe used some *honey* in the lemon mustard dressing to sweeten it. Bizarrely (based on what most kids like) he would also love some *marinated olives* scattered through. This is how I tend to think about adapting dishes for the 8yo. I think about his favourite things, and try to incorporate some of them – this gives him a 'comfort zone' and means a dish can be a jumping-off point for him to try other things he may be less comfortable with, potentially expanding his palate.

LAMB CHOPS with TAHINI CUCUMBER SALAD

Mix 2tbsp *tahini*, 2tbsp *natural yoghurt*, juice of 1 *lemon*, 1 crushed clove *garlic*, 1tbsp *olive oil*, *salt & pepper*. Add 1-3tbsp *water* to give desired consistency.

Chop ½ deseeded *cucumber* in half-moons. Dress cucumber with tahini sauce, scatter crumbled *feta* (optional) chopped *dill & mint*.

Rub *lamb chops* in *olive oil*, *thyme* leaves, *salt & pepper*.

Barbecue, ca. 3-4 min per side. Using tongs hold fat on grill to render.

This was the last barbecue I cooked at home for Sam. It might seem luxury to fire up the barbecue just to cook some chops, but it's very much the way we roll(ed). A barbecue should not always be about cooking as much as possible on the grill, it's about the flavour you can get into food by cooking it on fire. These lamb chops came from our local butcher, *M&K Butchers*, and simply cooked on the barbecue, they were just incredible – one of the tastiest things I have ever eaten. We served this with some homemade flatbreads also cooked on the barbecue. You can find the recipe on page 99, but instead of frying the flattened dough in the final step, just place it straight down on the barbecue – the flatbreads puff up and char beautifully.

CAKES and PUDDINGS

CHERRY EASY ROLY POLY

🐦 Mix 220g *SR Flour*, 110g *suet*, ca. 120ml *milk*, ½tsp *vanilla extract*. Form dough. Roll out ca. 30cm x 20cm.

Top with 4tbsp *cherry jam* leaving border.

Roll into long sausage, making sure cherries stay in roll.

Egg/milk wash, sprinkle 2tbsp *caster sugar* over.

Bake on lined baking tray, Fan 180, 35-40 min.

👤 I struggled for ages to get a jam roly poly recipe that I liked. Most require wrapping in a pleated parcel and steaming in the oven over a baking tray of water for up to an hour. Although it makes great roly poly, it is fiddly, and not very compatible with serving it as a Sunday lunch dessert. My oven is doing other stuff – I don't want it full of steam. And if I start the roly poly once everything is out of the oven, then we will be waiting an hour for pudding – trust me, the 8yo can't wait that long. This method is easy – no wrapping, no steaming. Make it in advance, then slide it into the oven 35-40 minutes before you need it. It's less of a 'steamed pudding', but on the flip side you get a sweet golden crust. The 8yo ate seconds, and asked for thirds, so it's a big win! The recipe serves 4 generously.

GREAT GRANDMA's SHERRY TRIFLE

For a small 17cm diameter trifle (ca. 1 litre).

Crush 6 *coconut ring biscuits*, place in bowl, spoon 35ml *Harvey's Bristol Cream sherry* over.

Cut 4 *trifle sponges* in half, generously spread *seedless raspberry jam* on cut side, put 2 layers in bowl, jam-side up. Spoon 65ml *sherry* over.

Make 280ml *Bird's custard* according to packet, pour over sponge when warm. Chill.

Whip 280ml *double cream* to soft peaks, spread on custard. Cling film over, leave 24 h. Top with flaked *almonds*.

This is guaranteed to provoke Twitter arguments – but it's a classic family recipe that can be traced back over 100 years to my Great Grandma. Controversially, this trifle has no jelly or fruit (it has raspberry jam). Sam always said this disqualified it from being a trifle. I like to think it's more like 'English tiramisu', with silky cream and custard, and an alcohol-soaked base. You can use shop-bought custard or make your own, but my family use 'Bird's'. My Mum's recipe in the photo, handed-on to me, is for double quantities. Trifle is a serious thing in her house, and it's always made in her best (2 litre) cut-crystal bowl. The secret ingredient is those coconut ring biscuits – they make the most amazingly addictive and unique bottom layer to this trifle – and if my Grandma called this a trifle, then a trifle it is!

PASSION FRUIT CURD BRIOCHE & BUTTER PUDDING

 Cut 175g *brioche loaf.*

Spread generously with *butter* & *passion fruit curd.*

Arrange in layers in baking dish adding *blueberries* as you go.

Whisk 200ml *milk*, 200ml *double cream*, 2 *eggs*, 25g *caster sugar*, zest of *lemon* & 1tbsp *lemon juice*, pour in tin, soak 30 min.

Place dish in tray part-filled with water. Bake, Fan 170, 30 min.

At the time, I couldn't find a brioche loaf to make this with, but we often have leftover brioche burger buns, so I used those, which explains why the photograph isn't the prettiest! However, this is a seriously tasty Bread & Butter Pudding. Like the recipe for Mum's Bread & Butter Pudding in *tw-eat* it uses the traditional method where the custard is not made in advance, although in this case, slightly more liquid is used to soak into the brioche. It's also richer than my Mum's original recipe because it uses cream as well as milk (it is the 21st century after all, not the 1970s). Once you have got the hang of this adaptation of Bread & Butter Pudding, which is largely the replacement of bread with brioche, raisins with blueberries and the addition of lemon curd, you can imagine many more. Why not spread the bread with jam or marmalade? Why not add raspberries, or stoned cherries? Bread & Butter Pudding is your canvas - make art!

ICED TRIPLE GINGER DRIZZLE CAKE

🐦 Gently melt 150g *butter*, 130g *molasses sugar*, 2tbsp *black treacle*, cool briefly. Add to 110ml *milk* in large bowl.

Mix in 2 beaten *eggs* and 3 pieces chopped *stem ginger*.

Add 225g *SR flour* & 1½tsp *ground ginger*, mix.

Spoon into *buttered* & lined 20cm cake tin. Bake, Fan 140, ca. 35 min.

Cool. Prick top of cake, drizzle with 1½ tbsp *syrup* from stem ginger.

Beat 100g *unsalted butter*. Slowly add 200g icing sugar, then 1tbsp *ginger syrup* & 2tsp *lemon juice* – use to frost top of cake.

👤 Simple and delicious, this is probably my favourite cake in the world. I love the frosting using the ginger syrup and the indulgent slightly sticky texture of the cake itself, combining stem & ground ginger for maximum flavour. As you can see from the photos, the 8yo helped me make this one. Working out baking quantities is a great way of developing kids' numeracy skills. You can also see it's something that Sam loved to do when he was very small!

BUTTERSCOTCH & BANANA HOT CROSS PUDDING

🐦 Tear up 3 *hot cross buns.*

Thick slice 2 *bananas.*

Mix in a lined loaf tin.

Melt 50g *butter*, add 80g *dark muscovado sugar*, 225ml *double cream* & 1tsp *vanilla extract*. Bring to boil for 2 min.

Pour over bun/banana mix.

Bake, Fan 180, 20-25 min.

👤 This is a variation on a *Nigel Slater* recipe – I just tweaked the sauce to turn it into a proper butterscotch and took quite a lot of sugar and cream out. At this scale, it fills the loaf tin and serves 4-6 people – you can always scale down. This pudding is not a looker, but it's got all the flavour! It's great if you want a child-pleasing pudding for practically no effort. It might turn out of the loaf tin after cooling a little, but really you may as well just scoop it out of the tin into bowls and greedily eat it hot with vanilla ice cream or a little cold double cream. This pudding is a regular, and popular, part of our Sunday lunches. As the 8yo said while he helped me make it: "You're making this again Daddy – I love it!!"

PLUM PIE

Rub 75g *butter* into 150g *flour* to breadcrumb texture. Add 50g *icing sugar* & 1 *egg yolk*. Form dough, add 1 tbsp *water* if needed. Chill in cling film, 30 min.

Stone & quarter 600g *plums*. Put in 20cm pie dish with 1 tbsp *caster sugar*.

Opt: add ¼ tsp ground spice (choose 1 of *cinnamon, cloves, star anise*).

Roll pastry, lay on pie. Brush with beaten *egg*, sprinkle *caster sugar*.

Bake, Fan 180, 25 min.

We grow plums on our allotment. This pie is just the best way to use them (apart from eating them straight from the tree). If you want to make it easier, you can buy sweet shortcrust pastry in super-markets, but the homemade pastry really makes it special.

A good fruit pie always reminds me of our 2016 family trip to America. In Shenandoah National Park, out in rural Virginia, we stayed at Skyland Lodge up on the mountain ridge. Each evening at dinner, we enjoyed spectacular views out over the forest. We always chose a traditional American fruit pie for pudding. I adore US National Parks – in Shenandoah, one hiking trip to a remote waterfall got interrupted by a black bear – a total highlight!

CELEBRATION VANILLA CAKE

 Cake

In large bowl, mix 225g *SR flour* & 2tsp *baking powder*. Then add 4 *eggs*, 225g soft *butter*, 225g *caster sugar*, ½tsp *vanilla extract* & 2tsp *milk*. Beat until smooth. (I use a stand mixer).

Spoon into two 20cm lined springform cake tins (350-400g in each).

Bake, Fan 140, 30-35 min until an inserted skewer comes out clean.

Leave in tins, 10 min, remove to cool.

Decoration

Slowly add 400g *icing sugar* to 200g *butter*. Mix well, then add ½tsp *vanilla extract* and ca. 2tsp *milk*.

Spread base of one cake with *raspberry jam*, base of other with buttercream. Sandwich together, buttercream cake on top.

Thinly spread top & sides of cake with buttercream.

Roll shop-bought *fondant icing*, overlay, trim base. Decorate.

This is a great recipe – it only takes about an hour, and the simple classic cake tastes fantastic (serves 12-16). To decorate, use a 20cm cake topper (as in the photo). These are edible prints you can buy online and stick to the icing – an easy way of delighting an 8yo. Alternatively, write on the iced cake with *coloured icing*, or don't ice it, just frost the top, and make a decorative pattern with *smarties*.

TOBLERONE CHEESECAKE

Crush 200g *chocolate digestive biscuits*, add 75g *melted butter*, press down in a 23cm buttered springform tin, chill.

Melt 200g *Toblerone* in bowl above pan of boiling water. Stir 200g *full fat cream cheese* until smooth. Mix the two together.

Whip 200g *double cream* to soft peaks, gently fold into chocolate mix.

Spoon onto biscuit base, chill. Decorate with extra *Toblerone* chunks.

Eurovision is the closest thing to a religion in this house – it's basically gay Christmas. My friends always organise parties, and they are invariably spectacular, with huge amounts of food. One year, we all took along food to represent a specific country – I drew Switzerland. Having toyed with the idea of a fondue and deciding it wasn't necessarily safe (given the large amounts of drink being consumed), I finally settled on this – a Toblerone cheesecake. By the way, this should come with a warning – there is not a single healthy ingredient in it. It is delicious though, and perfectly 'Eurovision kitsch'! You could also make a chocolate sauce to pour over it (melt 150g *dark chocolate,* 1tbsp *icing sugar,* 3tsp milk).

BLACKBERRY & LEMON TRIFLE

For a small 17cm diameter trifle (ca. 1 litre bowl).

Cut 200g *madeira cake* into cubes

Whip 350ml *double cream* with 25g *icing sugar* to soft peaks.

Crush 250g *blackberries* with 1tbsp *caster sugar* & 6 chopped *mint* leaves.

Layer the trifle: cream, cake, *lemon curd* (from jar, 50-100g), blackberries cream, cake, lemon curd (50-100g), blackberries, thick layer of cream.

Decorate with whole *blackberries*.

The perfect summer trifle combining fresh blackberries from the allotment, lemon curd, sponge and cream. This is something you can whip up quickly – it takes about 15 minutes. Like all trifles, it benefits from standing so that all the flavours come together and the cake absorbs the moisture, so leave it in the fridge for at least 2 hours. As an alcohol-free trifle, this is perfect for kids to enjoy, yet it's grown up enough for adults to appreciate as well.

BLACKBERRY & APPLE CRUMBLE TART

Peel & core 1 eating *apple*, cut into matchsticks.

Place 200g *blackberries* & the apple on a square of ready-roll *puff pastry*, leave border.

Mix 50g *flour*, 30g *rolled oats*, 60g *demerara sugar*, 40g melted *butter*. Lightly scatter over.

Brush border with beaten *egg*.

Bake, Fan 200, 25 min.

A very easy pudding combining the simple pleasures of tart and crumble. Sufficiently easy that it could mostly be made by the 8yo, this was a big hit. It's perfect served with vanilla ice cream. The crumble topping here is made in the way that Americans make 'Cobbler' using melted butter – you can do the melting in the microwave to make the cooking process even more 8yo-friendly.

SCARCROFT MESS

🐦 Halve 100g *cherries* and remove stones.

Cut 4 squares *homemade fudge* (page 111) into slivers & chunks.

Toast small handful *pistachios* in dry pan, then gently crush.

Fold most of ingredients through 150 ml *double cream* that has been whipped almost to stiff peaks.

Scatter remaining ingredients over top.

👤 Guaranteed to annoy one of my book critics who complained of my 'assembly' recipes, this is a very easy assembly pudding, and actually I'm very proud of it. It has everything you need, sweet fudge, fruity cherries, crunchy pistachios and softly whipped cream. Satisfaction in a bowl. Fundamentally, the concept is similar to an Eton Mess, only with the sweetness of the meringue replaced by fudge, and the meringue's crunchiness provided by pistachios. I've therefore named it after the area of York we live in – Scarcroft. The origins may be humbler than Eton, but I think it's just as good a pudding, and anyway, Etonians have been running things in the UK for far too long! You could of course use shop-bought fudge instead of homemade, but ideally, it should be slightly crystalline and not too soft. You can find my recipe for homemade fudge on page 111.

VANILLA CHRISTMAS VILLAGE

Cream 190g soft *butter*, 165g *caster sugar*, 1.5tsp *vanilla extract* with electric whisk.

Whisk in 3 *eggs*, 1 at a time.

Mix 190g *plain flour*, 1tsp heaped *baking powder*, pinch *salt*. Fold in.

Put in 1.4 litre 'Village' tin (it will rise to fill mould).

Bake, Fan 160, 30 min.

Cool, turn out. Dust with *icing sugar*.

When it comes to baking, I am more interested in flavour than appearance. However, baking with a Bundt tin is such a simple way to get beautiful bakes. I bought a 'Cozy Village' tin in the sale at a local cookshop, and now the snow-dusted 'Vanilla Village' has become our new Christmas tradition – described on Twitter by no-less than *Nigella* herself as 'so lovely'. The tin is only 1.4 litre capacity, so the cake is not too big – perfect for a small family. And it's just so festive to have a little snow-covered village in the kitchen from Christmas Eve through till Boxing Day – even if it is gradually getting eaten by a greedy 8yo and his dad. Sam loved Christmas kitsch – he would have adored this new tradition!

A LITTLE LONGER

SAM's CHINESE BEEF CHEEK STEW (& MANGO SALSA)

(🐦) Season 2 *beef cheeks*, fry in *oil* to brown.

Place beef in slow cooker (or casserole) and add 500ml *beef stock*, 3tbsp *soy sauce*, 3tbsp *Chinese rice wine* or *sake*, 2tsp *muscovado sugar*, *shiitake (or other) mushrooms*, 20g chopped *ginger*, 4 chopped *spring onions*, 2 *star anise*, pinch *cinnamon*.

Slow cook, 6-8 h. (Casserole, Fan 140, 3-4 h)

Briefly steam sliced *pak choi*, stir through stew, serve.

(👤) After I published *tw-eat*, Sam's mum sent me a WhatsApp message saying: "You may like to see this – it's the last meal Sam cooked for me. I asked him for the recipe and he wrote it out during his last days with us. He also got Stu to make it at home for him and bring it into the hospital, but he said it 'wasn't as good as his' – ha ha!"

In fact, this was a dish that was massively important to Sam,

> Diced Beef | Beef Cheek | Ruth
> Soy Sauce
> Chinese Rice Wine   Muscovado
> Beef Stock
> Ginger
> Spring Onions
> Mushroom (Fresh and/or Dry)
>
> Mix Sweetcorn
> Pak Choi
> Sugar Snap Peas
>
> Mango Salsa   Star Anise
> Mango
> Diced Onion
> Chilli   Cinnamon
> Coriander   Star Anise

possibly his signature dish, and it really should have been in Volume 1! It was something he would often cook for us on special occasions like New Year. I was delighted to rediscover it and seeing it in his own handwriting sent shivers up my spine.

The recipe uses beef cheek. If you've never had it, you must try. It responds fantastically to slow cooking, and delivers soft, tender, unctuous meat with a minimum of effort. You get a really generous portion of delicious beef. In this Asian stew the beef cheek takes on all of the fragrant flavours. Sam used to like this with mini sweetcorn, but they are something I just cannot stand – I prefer it with simple wilted pak choi – however Sam's other written suggestion of sugar snap peas is also good.

Although it's not at all Chinese, Sam liked to serve this dish with a *mango salsa* (1 *mango* peeled and chopped, 1 chopped *red chilli*, ½ *red onion* very finely chopped, juice of ½ *lime*, handful of chopped *coriander* leaves). Against the intense savoury flavours of the broth, the bright, zingy fruity flavours of this salsa lift everything – it's really very special.

The dish just needs some plain Jasmine rice to finish off. A few words on cooking *rice*. I always used to boil rice in a ton of water and drain it – I was never happy with the results. One of Sam's legacies is that he taught me how to cook rice properly, and it makes a massive difference.

<u>Rice</u>
Rinse rice in cold water, then add just the right amount of water, a little salt, bring to boil & cover.
Immediately turn down to very low heat, then turn off completely after about 5-10 min, so water slowly absorbs for perfect fluffy rice.
For *jasmine rice*, use 1½ cups of water for 1 cup of rice.
Basmati rice also uses 1½ cups of water for 1 cup of rice, but it benefits from soaking in water for 30 min prior to the rinsing step.
Japanese short grain (sushi) rice also needs soaking, but needs less water, so use 1¼ cups of water for 1 cup of rice.

Like many people in East Asia, I now use a rice cooker to control the heat perfectly – it's one of my favourite kitchen gadgets and takes the stress out of cooking rice.

LAMB & DATE TAGINE with FLATBREADS

 Tagine

Gently fry chopped *onion* in 10g *butter*.
Add ½tsp *ground ginger*, ¼tsp *cinnamon, black pepper*, 1 min.
Then add 400g *lamb shoulder*, brown.
Add 300ml *water*, 30g *chopped dates*, pinch *saffron*, ½tsp *salt*.
Put lid on, low heat, 90 min, top with water if needed.
Add 1tbsp *honey*, 1tbsp *lemon* juice, 100g *whole dates*, 10 min.
Serve with *flaked almonds* fried golden in butter & slivers of *preserved lemon* rind.

 Flatbreads

Mix 250g *bread flour*, 250g *plain flour*, 1½tsp *salt*, 1 heaped tsp *dried yeast*.
Add 1tbsp *olive oil*, 325ml warm water, knead (I use a mixer – it's a wet dough).
Place in oiled bowl. Cover 1-2 h until risen.
Knock back. Divide into 125g pieces. (Freeze any you don't need).
Roll out to thin 'circles' ca. 3 mm thick.
Fry in hot dry pan, 2-3 min. When large bubbles appear and bottom side is well coloured, flip, 1-2 min.

As I mentioned in *tw-eat*, the first holiday I took with Sam involved a road trip through the Atlas Mountains to the Moroccan desert. As we drove past the date palm groves, fabulous dates were being sold from the side of the road. When we arrived at our riadh on the northern fringes of the Sahara Desert, we were greeted with a wonderful lamb & date tagine. We sat together as the sun set, talking in the cool of the early evening – it felt so far from everyday life. Making this tagine transports me back there. Everywhere in Morocco, we had incredible food. There are also so many unique things to see and do – it's a hugely recommended trip if you enjoy good eating and adventure. I think it would be a fascinating family destination once the 8yo is old enough to really revel in the differences.

If you cook this tagine in a stovetop-safe casserole or tagine then the 90 min gentle heat section is better done in the oven (Fan 160), with the beginning and end of the cooking on the stovetop. Alternatively, you can put it in the slow cooker on low for 6-8 hours for this section of the cooking. If you want a 'meatier' texture, replace lamb shoulder with leg – the method remains the same. If you want more veg, throw in shredded *savoy cabbage* for the last 10 minutes with the dates. You might think it's not authentic, but when we stayed at an atmospheric riadh up in the Atlas Mountains in a restored crumbling ruin of a building, we were served cabbage tagine. We were secretly deeply unimpressed when told what was for dinner but had to eat our words – it was one of the most incredible things we ever tasted!

The flatbreads are brilliant and are a standard item in our kitchen. They go well with this tagine, but are also great with curries, stews, soups etc. There's nothing quite like tearing up warm fresh flatbread to dip in sauce. Each 125g flatbread serves one person. Once you have made a batch of dough, you can divide and freeze it – the quantities are enough to make 6 flatbreads. The dough, and concept, is *Hugh Fearnley Whittingstall's* (we use the same dough to make pizzas, see *tw-eat*). The cooking method sounds weird (raw dough in a frying pan), but trust me, it works! Once you have tried it, you will make sure you always have some dough in your freezer, and you won't ever buy vacuum packed flatbreads again. To flavour your bread, make an infused oil (e.g. gently heat crushed *garlic, rosemary* & *thyme* in *olive oil*), then tip it over the cooked bread.

HOMEMADE FISH FINGERS and 'CUSTARD'

🐦 Melt 20g *butter*, add 20g *flour*. Slowly add ca. 300 ml *milk*, stirring. Add 100g grated *cheddar*, *salt*, *white pepper* and 1tsp *Dijon mustard* (optional). Simmer 5 min.

Slice *cod fillets* into batons. Dip in *seasoned flour*, then beaten *egg*, then *panko breadcrumbs*.

Fry in thin layer of *sunflower oil* in pan, turning carefully until golden, ca. 5 min.

Serve with the 'custard' sauce, *peas* and *fries/chips*.

👤 The 8yo really loves Dr Who, which forms the inspiration for this dish. Famously, when the Doctor first regenerates as Matt Smith, he is starving hungry, and ransacks the kitchen of a young Amy Pond looking for something to eat. In a hilarious scene, nothing satisfies him until he alights on the combination of fish fingers and custard. In honour of that scene, which always makes the 8yo giggle, this dish was birthday tea on his 6th birthday. It was a particularly challenging birthday. Sam was extremely ill in hospital, and by this stage we all knew he was not going to recover. I had to put together something special to take the 8yo's mind off the endless string of hospital visits and the fact that everything was so uncertain. This birthday tea was crazy enough to take his mind off things and make us both laugh for an hour.

For that same birthday, he also had a trampolining party with his friends for which I made a 'Tardis' cake. Tempting as it is to include the recipe, I would not actually wish it on anyone to have to make it. Containing a spiced sponge within a decorated gingerbread shell, it took me about 6 hours of baking/decorating and would take several pages to describe. It is definitely not a '*tw-eat*' creation! However, the cake became symbolic of so much more than a birthday. I took the finished version to show Sam in his hospital bed. The cake

essentially said: "things are going to be ok… we are going to be ok… I've got this." Whatever I might have really been feeling inside, this is exactly what Sam (and the 8yo) needed to know at the time.

I love the Tardis photographs below. The 8yo and 'Jodie Whittaker' is taken in Madame Tussauds in Blackpool – one of his favourite museums in the world. The 8yo loves the Tardis – he even has an amazing Tardis wardrobe in his bedroom, created by talented friends. The other photo shows Sam as a young boy 35 years earlier, excitedly stood next to Davros. When a parent has died, links between generations take on extra resonance, they certainly help the 8yo feel closer to Sam. Some of my own most-prized childhood possessions are a Tardis & Tom Baker doll – nowadays they are collectors' items, but the 8yo loves to get them out and look at them – what good are memories if you don't use them and share them.

MAKI ROLLS

 Rice

Stand 100g *sushi rice* in water, 30 min, rinse.

Place in pan with 150ml *water* & 2tsp *mirin*. (Or in rice cooker)

Bring to boil, turn heat low, lid on, 10min. Turn heat off, 10min.

Add 20ml *rice wine vinegar*, mix gently. Put in bowl to cool.

Maki (makes 16-20)

Put 1 *nori sheet*, shiny side down, on rolling mat. Cover with ½ cooled rice, leaving far long edge clear.

Lay filling (e.g. *cucumber*, *crabstick*, *carrot*, *tuna mayo*, *avocado*, cooked *asparagus*, or mixtures) lengthways, left-to-right, ⅓ way up.

Roll away from you, brush far edge with *water*, squeeze to seal.

Slice roll into maki. Repeat with second nori sheet.

Serve with *soy sauce*, *wasabi* & *pickled ginger*.

Does the 8yo love sushi? I am convinced he could eat his body-weight in maki rolls. He can certainly eat his way through a significant portion of my salary in his favourite restaurant, *Yo Sushi*. He loves the little portions, the dipping sauces, the pickled ginger, and more than anything else, he loves the conveyor belt! Honestly, for the 8yo, the saying 'like a kid in a sweetshop' should be changed to 'like a kid in a sushi restaurant'.

In honesty, I find making sushi at home a bit of a pain – to my mind it's more of a craft than actual cooking, and I am hopeless at craft! It's something I really find quite stressful and difficult. Nonetheless, it is undoubtedly the way to the 8yo's heart, and so occasionally, making a batch of sushi rice and getting out the rolling mats and nori is a good way to spend an afternoon.

You can, of course, use *raw fish* in maki, but make sure you have a sushi-grade supplier. The best raw fish I ever ate was at my friend Jonny's house in Tokyo. His mother-in-law was Japanese; she made Sam and I the most incredible sashimi dinner to welcome us to Japan – as you can see from the photo, it was simply mind-blowing!

Making sushi is something Sam loved to do with the 8yo, it's something the 8yo's Nanny (Sam's mum) also enjoys. Sam made sure his maki were neat, to achieve this, you may need to trim the nori sheet down to avoid it 'folding in' on itself. You will also notice in the photograph there are some fancy 'inside-out' maki rolls, coated in black and white sesame seeds and with the nori tightly wrapping the filling. The batch of sushi in that photo was made by Sam with help from the 8yo (then a 5yo). Don't ask me how he did it – I have no clue. I mean, I could look it up and put it in the book, but sometimes it's just nicer to remember the man I married as some kind of sushi master rather than unmask all of the mysteries.

In fact, Sam (and his family) are all creative and artistic – it puts me to shame. In his final year of life, Sam took up a silversmithing class. One of my most precious possessions is the silver ring that he made in the studio – I keep it on a chain and wear it round my neck whenever I want to feel him close.

UNDERTALE BUTTERSCOTCH CINNAMON PIE

 Pastry

Rub 75g *unsalted butter* into 150g *plain flour*. Mix in 50g *icing sugar*.
Add 1 *egg yolk*, 1tbsp cold water, form dough. Wrap in cling film, chill.
Roll pastry, line 20cm fluted pie tin, prick.
Place greaseproof paper on pastry, add baking beans.
Bake Fan 160, 20 min. Remove paper & beans, Bake Fan 190, 20 min.

 Filling

Mix 4tbsp heaped *cornflour* & 3 *egg yolks*. Slowly whisk in 450ml *milk*.
Melt 25g *butter*, add 75g *light brown sugar*, boil 3 min. Add 180g *double cream*.
Slowly whisk egg/milk mix into cream mix.
Add ½tsp *cinnamon*, ¾tsp *salt*, bring to boil.
Remove from heat, stir in 50g *butterscotch chips* till melted.
Pour into pie case, cool in fridge.
Stiffly whip *double cream* with a little *icing sugar*, pipe to decorate.

The 8yo adores the computer game Undertale. In the game, one of the characters bakes you a Butterscotch Cinnamon Pie that can restore all your health points. So, one day, I decided to make the 8yo this as a special treat. I hacked the recipe together with ideas from several different places and it came out really well.

Sam loved computer gaming. One of the things he used to do with the 8yo was sit and play Lego Dimensions on the PlayStation – it was a team effort, controlling the action on the screen and also using the Lego figures on the action pad to activate different characters. After Sam died, I encouraged the 8yo to play some PlayStation games. It may sound like rubbish parenting, but the problem solving and determination required to succeed in games are good for him. It also provides worlds that he can escape to if he needs, and a space that is his, where he is the expert. Even better, in the case of the adventure game Undertale, playing it improved his reading far more than any Oxford Reading Scheme book had ever managed! I know that the 8yo sees gaming as a connection to Sam, and I think Sam would have been proud of him.

This is an American-style pie – although it sounds complicated, it's easy at heart. Make pastry, bake a pie case, make a filling, put the filling in the pie case and chill – there is no baking of the pie itself. You can make the recipe significantly easier by buying a sweet pie case from the supermarket. Then all you need to do is make the filling, pour it in and chill – you will then have your butterscotch cinnamon pie with about 15 minutes work. The butterscotch chips should completely melt into your filling – you don't want hard bits in the pie, all you are trying to do is boost the butterscotch part of the flavour profile. Some supermarkets sell butter-scotch chips, but if you are struggling to find them, bash some *butterscotch boiled sweets* (e.g. Werther's Original) until crushed into very small pieces, and stir them through the hot mixture. This pie is

surprisingly delicious, and I promise that even a small slice of it will make you feel like you have restored all of your health points.

HAM in VIMTO with CHERRY GLAZE

 Simmer *gammon* in *fizzy Vimto*, 50-60 min/kg.

Heat 130g *cherry jam*, 30g *golden syrup*, 30g *demerara sugar*, ½ cinnamon stick for 3-5 min, stir well. Cool.

Put cooked ham in foil-lined tin.

Score ham fat, stud with *cloves*.

Brush ham all over with cherry glaze. Roast, fan 220, 10-15 min.

In *tw-eat*, I wrote about my love for *Nigella Lawson's* Ham in Coca Cola, but also noted that I couldn't really move beyond it because it was so redolent with memories of Sam. Well, I finally did it, and Ham in Vimto with a Cherry Glaze was officially born! It's not that I've moved beyond Sam – I will never manage that, and nor will the 8yo. It was, however, partly the process of writing these books that helped me come to terms with my memories – organise them, collect them. Almost as if with a solid foundation of delicious food and wonderful memories, I could see a way forward. Anyway, this is easy, very tasty, and glazes the ham with a gorgeous red sheen. I suggest boiling the ham for 50 min/kg if it has been taken out of the fridge well before cooking, 60 min/kg if it is a large ham and still cold.

AFTERS

APEROL SPRITZ

Put several *ice cubes* and an *orange slice* in a short tumbler.

Add 50ml *aperol*, slowly add 75ml *prosecco*.

Top with *soda water* to taste (Sam's taste was for minimal).

I adore this photograph of Sam, taken in the late afternoon sunshine in Trieste, Italy. I was there on business, visiting my long-time collaborator and best scientific friend, Professor Sabrina Pricl. Her and Sam got on so well – their shared passion for good food, their unquenchable *joie de vivre*, and their love for a piece of gossip and a good story. We always planned to spend an extended period of time in Trieste, but eventually becoming dads stopped that from happening. I know there are few places Sam would rather be than somewhere in Italy, drinking an Aperol Spritz after a day exploring in the sun, while looking forward to some great food. Aperol spritz is a classic cocktail from exactly this region of North East Italy, but in recent years has increasingly become ubiquitous across the globe, to the point it barely needs a recipe. For a proper taste of *la dolce vita* with Sam, just follow the instructions above. Cheers!

STRAWBERRY GIN

Sterilise a large Kilner jar by heating in oven to 100°C.

Hull and slice 400g washed *strawberries*. Add 100g *caster sugar*. Add 700ml *London Dry Gin*.

Leave 3-4 weeks, gently inverting to mix every few days.

Strain through coffee filter into bottles for storage.

My good Twitter friend Stuart Cantrill, editor of one of the leading Chemistry journals, makes amazing fruit gins. When Sam passed away, Stu sent me a collection of his work in many different flavours. Every time I drank one, I felt a little bit more healed. Inspired by his expertise, I took on the challenge of a strawberry gin. It is a fantastic summer gin and has the benefit of being super quick to make – ready to drink in less than a month. The method here can be applied to any soft fruit. You can use exactly the same recipe for *blackberries*. In that case, although the gin can be drunk when it is decanted off the fruit, it continues to mature for 3 more months – perfect for a Christmas tipple. For sloe gin, double the sugar, and leave the gin to steep with *pricked sloes* for 3 months. That gin is ready for drinking in early spring. Pick your fruit wisely, and you can have a year-long supply of seasonal gins. Sam would have definitely approved!

BLACKPOOL VANILLA FUDGE

Mix 180g *caster sugar* & 50ml *milk*. Heat 2 min to dissolve

Add 160g *condensed milk*, ½ tsp *salt*.

Heat to boil. Boil/whisk 6 min Colour pale butterscotch (116-118°C)

Take off heat, add ½tsp *vanilla extract*. Whisk 1-2 min – it thickens.

Pour in lined loaf tin, rest 5-10 min, cut into ca. 18 pieces.

Blackpool is one of the 8yo's favourite places in the world - the lights, the trams, the sea, the amusements, the fish & chips... and we both love the fudge shop in the photograph. When I was a boy growing up in Stockport, we visited Blackpool Illuminations every year. Despite the fact some people sneer at Blackpool, and comment on its slightly tatty edges, I have always completely loved the place – the pure escapism and fun it represents. Now, each Autumn, the 8yo and I head to Blackpool for a few days of end-of-year fun. We stay in a hotel with a sea view and make a holiday of it. We both love the fact there is so much to do - Madame Tussauds, The Sandcastle, The Tower, The Pleasure Beach – we are never bored, and the 8yo is usually smiling. I also have an excellent track record of winning a cuddly toy on the racing camels.

This fudge brings a little taste of Blackpool back into our kitchen at home. The recipe is specifically for a small batch of fudge for a small family! It does keep in a tin for about 2 weeks (it gradually hardens). If you scale up the batch to use a whole can of condensed milk (400g), then you need 450g caster sugar (as you pour it out you can almost sense the onset of diabetes) and 125 ml milk. You will need to boil the mixture for a little longer – 8 minutes – check you've got the right temperature – it should be 116-118°C. You should then set the fudge in a 20cm square baking tin – it makes about 40 pieces.

Blackpool was the last family holiday we ever went on with Sam. By this stage he was really very poorly, and was struggling to walk. We hopped on and off the trams, tried to keep things chilled, and managed to have an absolutely lovely time. I remember us all sitting having a drink on the end of Central Pier on a beautiful late October afternoon. The sun was setting outside the windows and we had a view out over the Irish Sea. Our little family was all together and happy, but deep down, I knew that the sun really was setting, and that we probably would not be able to do this all together again.

RAINBOW MUFFINS with VANILLA FROSTING

 Muffins

Cream 125g *butter* with 125g *caster sugar*.
Beat in 2 *eggs*, 1 at a time, slowly adding 125g *SR flour* as you do so.
Add 1tsp *vanilla extract* and 3tbsp *milk*, mixing after each addition.
Divide into 6 bowls (ca. 75g per bowl).
Add *food colour gel* to each bowl: (i) purple (*red/blue*), (ii) *blue*, (iii) green (*blue/yellow*), (iv) *yellow*, (v) orange (*red/yellow*), (vi) *red*.
In 8 muffin cases load & gently spread 1 heaped tsp of each coloured mix from (i)-(vi) in order.
Bake, Fan 180, 15-20 min.

 Frosting

Beat 60g *butter*, 1 min. Add 1 tsp *vanilla extract*. Mix in 120g *icing sugar* in portions, and then add 2-3tsp *milk*. Beat until fluffy. Pipe onto muffins.

 Finally, after a long journey through the two volumes of *tw-eat*, I come to one of the happiest days of my life – the day I married Sam. We had a beautiful day with friends and family at *The Hospitium* in Museum Gardens, York. The sun shone, the sky was blue, and everything was right with the world. The most memorable food item was our cake. Long before rainbow cake was 'a thing' we decided we wanted a wedding cake with an ordinary exterior, but a rainbow interior – just like us. The first cake-maker we asked thought it was too difficult, the second was not interested in making a cake for a gay ceremony. Eventually, we found a wonderful local cake-maker, who embraced our vision. The rainbow cake has since become a baking classic, almost a cliché, but back then, it made the cutting of our cake a landmark moment.

This recipe remakes the idea of a rainbow cake in cupcake form. It's an easy bake, and fun to do with kids. However, be warned, it uses a lot of bowls, and loading the batter into the muffin cases gets messy. If you want layers, very gently spread each batter with the back of your teaspoon as you load it. If you want something more abstract just load the batter in splodges. First time I tried this, I used liquid food colours, but they bleached out to a muddy brown during the bake. Use extra strong gel colours designed for baking! You can buy every colour of the rainbow, but there's something fun about blending your own – if you have red, yellow and blue, you can mix the others.

Museum Gardens is a very special place for us. As well as having been married there, the 'Edible Wood' in the Gardens, which showcases edible plants, is the location of Sam's memorial bench. We scattered some of his ashes there and visit regularly. The 8yo loves exploring the gardens, and we often take something to eat and sit on Sam's bench for a while.

Some people think the story of our family is sad – that we have been unlucky. Others say Sam was lucky to have had us both. In fact, it was the 8yo and I who were lucky. Our lives are so much richer for having had Sam in them – anyone who knew him would understand. Things may have been hard, but it's far better to have had something remarkable than to have never had it at all. As I hope these books show, memory gives us strength and sustains us. As we reinvent memory into new traditions, like these rainbow muffins, the 8yo and I look to the future with optimism and togetherness.

INDEX

Printed in Great Britain
by Amazon

WILD FLOWERS OF SARK

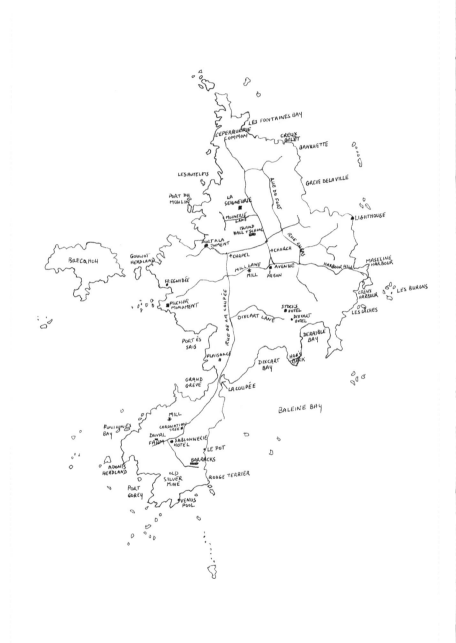

LES FONTAINES BAY

L'EPERQUERIE
COMMON

CREUX
BELET

BANQUETTE

LES AUTELETS

GREVE DE LA VILLE

PORT DU
MOULIN

LA
SEIGNEURIE

RUE DU FORT

MOINERIE
LANE

ISLAND
HALL + SCHOOL

LIGHTHOUSE

PORT A LA
JUMENT

RUE LACHES

BRECQHOU

GOULIOT
HEADLAND

+CHAPEL

+CHURCH

MASELINE
HARBOUR

MILL LANE

AVENUE

HARBOUR HILL

FREGONDÉE

MILL

PRISON

CREUX
HARBOUR

LES BURONS

PILCHER
MONUMENT

RUE DE LA COUPÉE

DIXCART LANE

STOCKS
HOTEL

LES LACHES

DIXCART
HOTEL

PORT ÈS
SAIS

DERRIBLE
BAY

PLAISANCE

HOG'S
BACK

DIXCART
BAY

GRAND
GREVE

LA COUPÉE

BALEINE BAY

MILL

PUNIHOU'S
BAY

CORONATION
TREE

DUVAL
FARM

SABLONNERIE
HOTEL

LE POT

BARRACKS

ADONIS
HEADLAND

OLD
SILVER
MINE

ROUGE TERRIER

PORT
GOREY

VENUS
POOL

Wild Flowers
of Sark

Susan Synnott

ELSP

Published in 2011
by ELSP
11 Regents Place
Bradford on Avon
Wiltshire   BA15 1ED

Origination by Seaflower Books
www.ex-librisbooks.co.uk

Printed and bound in Britain by
Butler Tanner and Dennis Ltd, Frome, Somerset

ISBN 978-1-906641-25-2

**All correspondence and enquiries regarding
this book should be addressed to**

**Susan Synnott
La Cloture de Bas
Sark
Channel Islands
GY10 1SD**

CONTENTS

Path to Grève de la Ville

ACKNOWLEDGEMENTS

My sincere thanks to Dr Roger Veall, my botanical advisor and mentor, who has shared his wealth of knowledge and expertise with me, to Dr Richard Axton for his advice and encouragement and for the many happy botanical outings with him and his wife, Marie, to Caroline Langford who sparked off the idea for a handbook in the first place, to Penny Prevel for her Spring wild flower walks which have much inspired me, to the many Sark residents who have drawn my attention to plants in odd places, including Shân Bache, Jo Birch, Shirley Carré, Sue Daly, Linda Higgins, Ronnie Stokes, and Sally Ward-Jones to name but a few, to the property owners over whose land I have spent many happy hours searching for plants, to my publisher Roger Jones at Seaflower Books for his help and encouragement in this project. Last but not least I would like to thank my husband David for his unfailing patience at my interest in what he calls 'glubjumbos'!

Towards L'Eperquerie

INTRODUCTION

When I first came to Sark nine years ago I was amazed at the plant life here. Not knowing much about plants, garden or otherwise, I decided that I would like to have some idea about what I was passing on my bicycle every day between Little Sark and the village. Inspired by the first Wild Flower Fortnight in April 2004 (a yearly event ever since) led by Tourism Officer Penny Prevel with the expert help of Dr Roger Veall, I got to learn many of the plants in our midst. For many years Roger and Psyche Veall have been visiting regularly from England to study Sark's plants. In between the Vealls' visits I have also spent many happy hours botanising with Dr Richard and Dr Marie Axton, usually finishing our walk at one of the lovely tea gardens dotted around the island! Taking photographs has been very useful in helping me to remember the plants more easily, but there is still so much to learn.

It has become popular in recent years to have a wild flower garden. But Sark is a showcase of wild flowers growing naturally as, unlike in other parts of the world, Sark has never gone in for intensive farming. The hedgebanks have been retained, the fields are small and irregular, the borders of the fields have been left to nature, and our cliff tops are undeveloped. Some of Sark's plants are native, but others have been introduced either through crop seed, birdseed, and/or garden plants which have escaped, e.g. the impressive Elecampane (*Inula helenium*) now found on the roadside outside La Ville Roussel or the immensely tall Echiums which appear throughout the island. These and other incomers are now very much part of our landscape. Much of Sark is a wildflower garden without human input; it is part of its special charm.

This is not a comprehensive list of plants on Sark, but a selection of the commonest ones and some not so common which hold special interest for me. Some plants are tiny with flowerheads the size of a pin head. The exquisite design of these little flowers, such as Bird's-foot *(Ornithopus perpusillus)*, never ceases to amaze me, and there are many others. As Sark is such a small island nowhere is far from the sea yet some plants can be very much reduced in size on cliffs compared to a similar species more inland to cope with the bracing, salt laden winds. Familiar faces appear each year, but then some plants come and go and don't reappear for several years or perhaps never, or in a very different location. Recently Greater

9

Celandine (*Chelidonium majus*) has reappeared near Nat West Bank after an absence of nearly twenty years. Early-purple Orchid (*Orchis mascula*) has also been re-discovered in a different location to where it had been seen in the 1980s. This is the fascinating thing about botany, it is full of surprises and you never know what you might find when you go for a walk. I have even found a 'first' for Sark on my very doorstep at the Barracks, an Annual Wall-rocket *(Diplotaxis muralis)* growing on the paving outside my front door!

I found it difficult to decide how best to categorize the plants chosen. By family can be very useful so as to familiarize a person to the common characteristics but I have decided against that. Arrangement by habitat has much to commend it, but many of our habitats on Sark overlap being such a small island. By season is not always helpful as plants can extend their flowering time into the next season, or reappear out of season: I have seen Primroses and Violets in November.

In the end I decided to categorize by colour as this booklet is really a quick reference guide and not an in-depth botanical study. Some plants have a variety of colours, e.g. Common & Heath Milkwort (*Polygala vulgaris & P. serpyllifolia)* but the most usual colour form seen is blue so I have put them in the blue section. I have also kept all the Cudweeds together in the white colour section as the most common one noticed is Cape Cudweed *(Gnaphalium undulatum)* which has whitish flowers and the other cudweeds are less often noticeable, even though Common Cudweed *(Filago vulgaris)* has more yellowish flowerheads. The colour sections are very general, yellow, white, pink, blue, and green with variations within a section, e.g red in the pink section.

However at the top of each page I give the family to which that particular plant belongs. Each plant's name is in English as well as the scientific name in Latin as common names can vary depending on locality. The Latin name helps standardize naming throughout the world. For example the common name *Lesser Trefoil* is known in other places as *Suckling Clover*, and in Ireland is considered to be the *Shamrock*, but the scientific name is *Trifolium dubium* regardless from where it comes.

Family and plant names have changed in recent years. With the introduction of DNA sequencing of plants in the 1990s relationships between certain plants have changed and therefore their classification. Thale Cress (*Arabidopsis thaliana*) was the first plant genome sequenced as it has a small number of chromosomes, 10, compared to 14 for Rye or 48 for cultivated tobacco. I have attempted to bring the plant names and the sequencing of plants in each colour section in this hand book as up to date as possible using Clive Stace's *Flora of the British Isles*, 3rd edition which was published in March 2010.

I have also concentrated on flowering plants and do not include grasses, trees or ferns. A separate booklet on *Ferns of Sark* is available from La Société Sercquaise. For a comprehensive list of all uncultivated flowering plants including trees, grasses and ferns of Sark Roger Veall's *Plants of Sark* is certainly advisable. I would also recommend the field companion *Flowers of Sark* by Anne Allen with wonderful detailed drawings by Barbara Hilton, which has a more detailed description of plants in their habitats, a guide to plant families, and is all colour coded. These two publications are available from the Gallery Stores. They are also available to the public for browsing at La Société Sercquaise centre along with many other books and pamphlets of botanical interest. The centre also houses our Herbarium which was started by Marcia Marsden in 1980 who meticulously mounted specimens for posterity but who, unfortunately, died in early 2004 before I had time to really know her. The Herbarium has over 550 specimens and is constantly updated.

Susan Synnott
Sark, March 2011

Spring afternoon, Rue de la Coupée

Poppy Family – Papaveraceae

Greater Celandine

Chelidonium majus

There is no relationship between this and Lesser Celandine (Buttercup Family) as it is from a very different family, the Poppy family. Medium perennial to 90cm, the flowers with 4 yellow non-overlapping petals, 15-25mm. Leaves hairless, toothed and very divided. Has reappeared near Nat West Bank by the roadside in spring 2009 after an absence of almost twenty years.

Buttercup Family – Ranunculaceae

Bulbous Buttercup

Ranunculus bulbosus

A common buttercup from March-June. One of the earliest to appear in drier grassland. Erect perennial to 40cm, shorter than Meadow Buttercup. Glossy yellow flowers with 5 petals, 15-30mm, and sepals turned down. Hairy, the leaves with 3 main lobes, the middle one stalked.

Meadow Buttercup

Ranunculus acris

Not very frequent in Sark. One of the tallest buttercups, up to 1m, in damper meadows. A hairy perennial, with yellow glossy flowers, 15-25mm. Sepals erect or spreading as the flower opens. Long, unfurrowed stalks with basal leaves palmate and deeply cut, middle lobe unstalked unlike Bulbous and Creeping Buttercup. Appears a little later than the Bulbous Buttercup, from May.

Buttercup Family – Ranunculaceae

Left: Bulbous Buttercup

Right: Creeping Buttercup

Creeping Buttercup

Ranunculus repens

Sepals erect like Meadow Buttercup but a shorter plant with creeping runners, and furrowed stalks. Leaves in 3 lobes with middle lobe stalked. Very common in grassy habitats from April.

Buttercup Family – Ranunculaceae

Lesser Celandine

Ficaria verna

One of the first signs of spring when these cheerful yellow flowers grace the hedgerows and grassland from February onwards. Not very tall, up to 30cm, hairless, solitary flowers with 7-12 narrow, glossy, yellow petals, tinged bronze underneath, and 3 sepals. Leaves dark green, heart-shaped and long stalked.

Road to Gouliot Headland with Lesser Celandines

Stonecrop Family - Crassulaceae

Navelwort

Umbilicus rupestris

The leaves are mostly basal, very fleshy, rounded, with a navel-like dimple in the centre, hence its name. They appear first before the long spikes of greenish-yellow, bell-shaped flowers. Grows up to 50cm and is very common in various habitats, roadsides, coastal areas, Harbour Hill and even on a tree opposite the Assembly Room! Also known as Wall Pennywort.

Navelwort on cliff path near old silver mine, Little Sark

Pea Family – Fabaceae

There are many varieties from the Pea family (Fabaceae) in Sark with their distinctive flowerheads, 5 petalled, the broad standard at the top, with 2 narrower wings at the side, and the two lowest petals joined as the keel. The leaves are usually pinnate or trefoil. The fruit usually resembles a pea pod.

Common Bird's-foot-trefoil

Lotus corniculatus

This is the most common and is seen from spring onwards, up to 50cm in height. Sometimes known as 'bacon and eggs' because of the red streaks through the yellow petals in clusters of 2-7. Pods are like a bird's foot hence part of its name, and 'trefoil' refers to three leaflets together, but it has an extra pair of leaves at stalk base. Found on grass, roadside banks etc.

Pea Family – Fabaceae

Greater Bird's-foot-trefoil

Lotus pedunculatus

A larger plant than Bird's-foot-trefoil, with thicker, hairy, hollow stems to 1m and darker green leaves. Flowers rich yellow, 5-12 clustered in a head. Fairly frequent in Sark in damper areas. Specimens in photos near La Vaurocque and La Jaspellerie.

Pea Family – Fabaceae

Kidney Vetch

Anthyllis vulneraria

Less frequently seen but it appears from late May. Different from Common and Greater Bird's-foot Trefoil in that its yellow flowerheads are kidney-shaped with downy-white sepals and leafy bracts. Thought in the old days that this plant could cure kidney diseases, hence its common name. Grows to 60cm. Leaves fleshy, the upper ones with 4-5 pairs of leaflets. Seen near the sea at La Coupée, Les Fontaines in Little Sark, and Derrible and Dixcart Bay.

Lone Kidney Vetch at La Coupée

Pea Family – Fabaceae

Hairy Bird's-foot-trefoil

Lotus subbiflorus

and

Slender Bird's-foot-trefoil

Lotus angustissimus

Hairy and Slender Bird's-foot-trefoils are not seen as often as Common Bird's-foot-trefoil. Both are hairy, but Slender is more downy with only 1-2 flowers in a head, keel petal right-angled and long slender pods, 12-30mm, whereas Hairy has 2-4 flowers in a head, is very hairy, its keel more obtuse and pods only 6-12mm. Both occasionally seen in similar habitats, dry grassland near the coast.

Pea Family – Fabaceae

Hop Trefoil

Trifolium campestre
and
Lesser Trefoil

Trifolium dubium

Hop and Lesser Trefoils are quite similar in appearance, both are low growing, but Hop Trefoil has a larger, globular flowerhead, 10-15mm, is a paler yellow and is more downy. Its seed is in the shape of a hop. Lesser Trefoil's flowerhead is only about 3-4mm. Leaves on both trifoliate. Both are fairly common on Sark and grow on grassy places near the sea and roadsides.

Looking towards Les Autelets

Pea Family – Fabaceae

Gorse

Ulex europaeus

A very familiar shrub brightening the landscape most of the year but at its best in spring. Bright yellow, coconut-scented pea-type flowers on woody stems with furrowed spines. Also known as Furze; it was used for fuel in Sark long ago.

Rose Family – Rosaceae

Tormentil

Potentilla erecta ssp. erecta

A slender, sprawling perennial with yellow flowers, 7-11mm, and 4 slightly notched petals. Stem leaves mostly divided into 3, toothed, with a pair of stipules at the base of short petiole (leaf stalk). Can be seen from May onwards on grassland and heaths. Especially visible up Harbour Hill pedestrian walk, and on heath near Vermandaye, Little Sark.

Trailing Tormentil

Potentilla anglica

Less frequent, Trailing Tormentil has 4-5 yellow petals with lower stem leaves split into 3-5 leaflets. Has recently been seen on the steps down to Les Fontaines Bay, Little Sark.

Rose Family – Rosaceae

Wood Avens (Herb Bennet)

Geum urbanum

A perennial from the Rose family. Considered as a charm against evil spirits in 15thcentury. This medium sized plant to 70cm has 5 unnotched petalled flowers, narrow sepals which turn down, and hairy stems. Basal leaves pinnate with end lobe the largest. Stem leaves 3-lobed. Fruits very distinctive, a bur-like head with hooked spines. Sometimes found along hedgerows in shady areas. In Sark seen along Moinerie Lane, Harbour Hill path, Port du Moulin and Dixcart wood.

Wood-sorrel Family – Oxalidaceae

Procumbent Yellow-sorrel

Oxalis corniculata

Also known as Spreading Yellow-sorrel as it spreads easily in garden beds, on gravel etc., with its creeping stems and deep roots. Flowers yellow, 6-10mm, with five petals. Leaves trifoliate and notched, often tinged purple.

Least Yellow-sorrel

Oxalis exilis

Another sorrel found on short grass, this is smaller with very frail stems, solitary yellow flowers and green leaves. Less common but has been seen on short grass at Pointe Robert, La Seigneurie gardens, and Maison Pommier.

St John's Wort Family – Hypericaceae

Slender St John's-wort

Hypericum pulchrum

Can be found on grassy banks, i.e. on pedestrian path up Harbour Hill, also open woods and heaths. It has slender, upright and hairless stems to 60cm. The flowers, 14-15mm, with yellow petals tinged red underneath. Petals and sepals have marginal black dots. Leaves triangular to ovate, half-clasping the stem with translucent dots.

Trailing St John's-wort

Hypericum humifusum

As the name describes it trails on the ground, has 2 ridged stems, yellow flowers, 8-10mm, with some black dots. Leaves are ovate to lanceolate. Occasionally found, usually on acid soil. Has been seen on L'Eperquerie common, Vallon D'Or and by the tennis court.

Weld, south of the Barracks, Little Sark

Mignonette Family – Resedaceae

Weld

Reseda luteola

A tall hairless perennial, up to 1.5m, with long spikes of yellow-green flowers. Leaves dark green, narrow, untoothed and slightly wavy edged. Has recently been seen near the dolmen on Little Sark and La Rondellerie near the coast. Other places seen are Derrible headland and above Dixcart Bay and in 2008 many seen in field south of the Barracks. Used in Medieval Age as a dye for yellow; 3-6 lbs of Weld plants needed to colour 1 lb of cloth.

Cabbage Family – Brassicaceae

Annual Wall-rocket

Diplotaxis muralis

Found originally at ports from ballast, but also a bird-seed alien. First seen in Sark in 2006 on cobbles at the Barracks, Little Sark. Also known as Stinkweed because of the unpleasant smell when the stem is crushed. Cruciform yellow flowers with cylindrical seed pods parallel to the stem, but at an angle, with 2 rows of seeds in each pod. Can grow to about 60cm. Leaves mostly in a basal rosette.

Cabbage Family – Brassicaceae

Hedge Mustard

Sisymbrium officinale

One of the many 'crucifer' plants in Sark with 4 petals shaped like a cross. Stiff stems up to 1m, the yellow flowers in clusters with short, cylindrical pods pressed along the stem. Leaves in basal rosette, deeply lobed, but with occasional narrow leaves on stem. Occasional on waste ground, hedgerows, and some arable fields. Specimen in photo near La Vaurocque. Recommended as a gargle if you lost your voice, according to Racine, a 17th century French dramatist.

Primrose Family – Primulaceae

Primrose

Primula vulgaris

Most people need no introduction to the Primrose, which heralds in the first signs of spring in the countryside, along hedgerows and in wooded areas. These solitary pale yellow flowers with notched petals and a deep yellow centre usually bring brightness and light after dark winter evenings. There are two types of flower, either stigma below the anthers 'thrum-eyed' or above 'pin-eyed' to help cross fertilization.

Bedstraw Family – Rubiaceae

Lady's Bedstraw

Galium verum

This bedstraw has tiny bright yellow 4-petalled flowers in clusters. Upright or sprawling with many branched square stems, found in pastures or on hedgerows from June. The undivided, narrow leaves of the bedstraw family are in whorls around the stem. Can smell of hay when dried and legend has it that it got its name from the Virgin Mary allegedly lying on a bed of it. The flowers were once used to curdle milk and for cheese-making. Common in Sark, with good patches near La Coupée or by Pilcher Monument, for example.

Speedwell Family – Veronicaceae

Common Toadflax

Linaria vulgaris

Mostly seen on roadsides or grassy banks in Sark from June onwards. Can grow up to 80cm but usually shorter. Yellow flowers in spikes each with an orange bulge and a long spur. Linear leaves arranged spirally up the stem. Can be seen on the road to Little Sark, on Mill Lane, and on a grassy bank in old graveyard by Methodist Church as well as other areas.

Dead-nettle Family – Lamiaceae

Wood Sage

Teucrium scorodonia

The pointed, oval, toothed and wrinkled leaves of this plant appear earlier than the flowers in spring, and are readily seen on hedgerows, roadsides, woods and even coastal areas. Flowers in spikes, pale greenish-creamy yellow, with a five lobed lower lip, the middle one spreading and no upper lip, so 2 brown stamens are uncovered. Grows up to 50cm. Apparently in Jersey it was used for brewing as it helped to clarify beer very quickly and gave the liquid a strong colour.

Broomrape Family – Orobanchaceae

Yellow Bartsia

Parentucellia viscosa

This upright, hairy plant to 50cm, has yellow flowers with a 'hood', and longer divided lower lip which appears at leaf axils.   Leaves lanceolate, toothed and unstalked, in pairs up the stem. Can be found in grassy places, especially damp areas, from June. Seen in fields near Jaspellerie, field behind the Gallery, and Creux Belet area and is fairly common.

Daisy Family – Asteraceae

Heath Groundsel

Senecio sylvaticus

Taller than Groundsel, to 70cm, with conical yellow disc-florets and short ray-florets, the rays soon curl under. Leaves yellowy-green, very deeply lobed on hairy stems, the upper ones stalkless (sessile). Found in Sark on heath, gravely places and sometimes on coastal walks. Groundsel was a popular food for caged birds when I was young; perhaps it is still today.

Daisy Family – Asteraceae

Smooth Cat's-ear

Hypochaeris glabra

Appears from late April in grassy places and on sandy soil. Low growing and sometimes sprawling. Flowerheads solitary, 10-15mm across, opening widely in full sun. Stems with a few scale-like bracts. Leaves in basal rosette, shiny and almost hairless. Has been seen at L'Eperquerie, west side, cliff path from silver mines towards Duval, and other places.

Daisy Family – Asteraceae

Cat's-ear

Hypochaeris radicata

Solitary yellow flowerheads, 25-40mm, with scales between the rayed-florets all surrounded by rows of dark tipped bracts. Short scale-like bracts, thought to resemble cat's ears, up the leafless stem. Can grow to 60cm. Leaves in basal rosette, oblong, lobed or toothed, and hairy. From spring onwards along roadsides and in meadows. Very common.

Daisy Family – Asteraceae

Ploughman's-spikenard

Inula conyzae

This tall, hairy perennial to 1 metre has been seen in Sark on the path down to Grand Grève, now closed to the public, and path to Derrible Bay. Until recently it was very rare but it now seems to be establishing itself in these two places. Small yellow flowerheads, 9-11mm, in loose umbel like clusters with green/purple bracts. Leaves lanceolate, upper ones unstalked, lower leaves larger, not unlike Foxglove leaves.

Daisy Family – Asteraceae

Elecampane

Inula helenium

An example of a striking garden escape from La Ville Roussel garden which is now happily settled along the roadside outside the boundary walls. Grows very tall to 2.5m with bright large yellow flowers with narrow ray-florets in July/August. Leaves also very large up to 40cm which appear earlier in the season.

Daisy Family – Asteraceae

Golden-samphire

Inula crithmoides

Erect, hairless perennial to 1m, with numerous fleshy, green, narrow leaves along the stem with single golden yellow daisy-like flowerheads at the top of branched stems. Found on cliffs. Has been seen on east side of La Coupée and near Venus Pool, growing with its unrelated Rock Samphire, and on other rocky ground near the sea, from July.

L'Etac, with Golden-samphire and Rock samphire in foreground

Daisy Family – Asteraceae

Corn Marigold

Glebionis segetum

Large bright yellow flowerheads, 35-55mm, like a large daisy, but with both rayed and disc-florets yellow. Grows up to 80cm. Leaves slightly fleshy and toothed, clasping the stem. A wonderful display has been seen in Little Sark on the west side in a small, triangular field near Coronation tree from June and in the north west of road to L'Eperquerie. Found mostly in arable fields.

Daisy Family – Asteraceae

Common Fleabane

Pulicaria dysenterica

A hairy perennial with yellow daisy-like flowers with both disc and ray-florets, 15-30mm, the yellow rays very numerous and the disc-florets a deep yellow. Basal leaves oblong and soon wither. Stem leaves heart or arrow-shaped, wavy, clasping the stem, and downy underneath. Pulicaria comes from Latin, pulex meaning flea as the leaves when dried and burnt helped to ward off fleas, apparently. Found in damp areas from August to September. Has been seen on Harbour Hill and Rue Lucas opposite telephone exchange, and other places.

49

Daisy Family – Asteraceae

German-ivy

Delairea odorata

 Originally from South Africa as a garden plant but has escaped. First seen in Sark in 1997 on a compost heap at Dixcart Hotel by Dr RM Veall. Since then it has been recorded near Dixcart Hotel by incinerator and also south of the first common on the left on the way to Venus Pool and at La Seigneurie gardens compost heap. A scrambling, woody plant with succulent leaves. Yellow flowerheads, 5-7mm, in dense terminal clusters which flower in November/December.

Honeysuckle Family – Caprifoliaceae

Honeysuckle

Lonicera periclymenum

Found in hedgerows in Sark and gives a wonderful scent, especially in summer evenings. Exotic looking flowers, 2- lipped with a narrow tube in terminal heads, creamy yellow, darkening after pollination, by bees in daytime, by moths at dusk. Leaves oval, untoothed and opposite. Glossy scarlet berries in autumn. Also know as Woodbine.

Ivy Family – Araliaceae

Atlantic Ivy

Hedera hibernica

Ivy clings to walls, trees, old buildings etc, with its familiar evergreen, shiny, leathery, triangular, sometimes lobed leaves. The flowers are very distinctive in globular, yellow-green umbels pollinated by wasps. Fruit is a purplish black berry. All ivy on Sark is Atlantic Ivy (*Hedera hibernica*) as it is now regarded as a full species. It used to be considered a subspecies of Hedera helix called *H. helix ssp. hibernica*. Other common names have been Western Ivy or Canary Ivy. A cultivated version for gardens is also Hedera 'hibernica' known either as Irish or Canary Ivy. *Hedera helix ssp. helix* (Common Ivy) is not found in Sark. Ivy and holly are used to decorate houses at Christmas but in old folklore ivy was used to ward off house goblins.

Carrot Family – Apiaceae

Rock Samphire

Crithmum maritimum

A member of the umbellifer family which has very fleshy leaves and grows very much by the sea from July to September. Short and bushy to 45cm with yellow/green umbel flowerheads. The common name 'samphire' is a corruption of the word 'Saint-Pierre' meaning St Peter who was the patron saint of fishermen and also known as the 'rock'. In the 17th century Sark had a good samphire trade, pickled and shipped from Guernsey to France and England. Gathering of it was a dangerous occupation as it mostly grows on cliffs. Shakespear's King Lear refers to the trade "Half way down hangs one that gathers samphire, dreadful trade".

Yellow Iris at Creux Belet

Iris Family – Iridaceae

Yellow Iris

Iris pseudacorus

Found in damper areas especially Creux Belet and also recently by Beauregard pond. Yellow flowerheads, linear green leaves and seeds yellowish/brown. Clovis, King of the Franks in late 5th century was the first to use the Iris on a heraldic device; the fleur-de-lis (Lily flower) is a stylised version of this plant.

Poppy Family – Papaveraceae

White Ramping-fumitory

Fumaria capreolata ssp. capreolata

This particular subspecies of Fumaria capreolata is the only one seen on Sark but is not as frequent as the *Fumaria muralis*, page 102. Scrambles over hedgerows or on disturbed ground. Has spikes of white tube-like flowers tipped with purple with up to 20 flowers on each spike. Leaves very slender and tangled. Has been seen near Le Carrefour and also down lane east of the Mill.

Stonecrop Family – Crassulaceae

White Stonecrop

Sedum album

A short perennial to about 20cm, with white flowers, 6-9mm, in domed clusters at tip of stem. Succulent, green, sometimes reddish oval leaves alternatively up the stem. This plant is not as common as the other stonecrops, but has been found outside the old forge at Plaisance, on a wall near La Valette, at La Rondellerie and near HSBC bank. There is also some growing in the bed at La Coupée carriage park, but this would have been planted.

Pea Family – Fabaceae

Bird's-foot

Ornithopus perpusillus

A very tiny plant which can hardly be seen with the naked eye, but with good sight the tiny pale white, streaked pink flowers can just about be seen in short grass. Slender, downy and sprawling to 30cm, the flowerheads, 3-5mm. Leaves with many leaflets. I always find it thrilling to see it as most people would never notice it at all, and certainly I wouldn't have either until I became aware of it a few years ago. Has been seen at La Banquette, Saut à Juan, Derrible headland and other places.

Pea Family – Fabaceae

White Clover

Trifolium repens

A very common sprawling, hairless perennial with white flowers, 7-12mm, sometimes pinkish, but browning with age on long stems. Leaflets rounded, toothed and trifoliate with usually a white mark on each leaf and translucent veins. A very good source of nectar for bees.

Pea Family – Fabaceae

Subterranean Clover

Trifolium subterraneum

Also called Burrowing Clover because the barren flowers in a flower-cluster 'burrow' by means of their hooked calyces into the ground. Low-growing, sprawling, hairy plant to 20cm. Flowers white, 8-14mm long, in clusters of 2-5. Leaves trifoliate with notched leaflets. Found on grass. i.e by War memorial in front of church, field west of Jaspellerie, bank near Gouliot headland and in turf west of La Fregondée. Can be confused with Bird's-foot Clover (*Trifolium ornithopodioides*), (not illustrated), which is not hairy.

Near Derrible Headland

Rose Family – Rosaceae

Burnet Rose

Rosa spinosissima

Low growing to 30cm in bushy patches. Flowers creamy white, 3-5cm, rarely pink, fragrant, solitary, with numerous straight prickles on stems. Leaves 7-9 rounded leaflets. Hips dark purple with undivided sepals persisting. Flowers May – July. Has been seen near La Coupée by the old cannon and near bench on the south side, also Adonis headland.

L'Eperquerie

Cabbage Family – Brassicaceae

There are two cress types of plants which are fairly common in Sark and which look quite similar. **Wavy Bitter-cress** (*Cardamine flexuosa*) and **Hairy Bitter-cress** (*Cardamine hirsuta*). However, Wavy Bitter-cress is found in damper areas, e.g. Dixcart Valley, Harbour Hill path, also near La Ville Farm and has a zig-zag type stem, up to 50cm, the tiny flowers having 6 stamens, whereas Hairy Bitter-cress is upright, grows to about 30cm, with its seed pods overtopping the flower cluster at the top of the stem. Its 4-petalled flowers have only 4 stamens and is very common in drier areas, bare ground, fields, roadsides. Both have pinnate leaves.

Cabbage Family – Brassicaceae

Danish Scurvygrass

Cochlearia danica

A very common plant in early spring to 20cm, along grassy paths near the coast. It has tiny groups of 4-petalled white or sometimes violet coloured flowers at the top of the stem. Leaves are glossy and stalked, the basal leaves heart-shaped, the upper leaves ivy-shaped. Fruits egg-shaped. Scurvygrass is rich in Vitamin C; formerly used to prevent scurvy, especially prevalent on long sea voyages.

Cabbage Family – Brassicaceae

Shepherd's-purse

Capsella bursa-pastoris

Found on waste ground and is very common. So called because of the shape of its seed pod which is meant to resemble a shepherd's purse of long ago, with its flattened, triangular shape. Very distinctive.

Thale Cress

Arabidopsis thaliana

Another cress seen occasionally. Has upright hairy stems, to about 30cm, and tiny white flowers in a cluster at the top. Most leaves in basal rosette, oblong, stalked and sometimes toothed, but some stem leaves unstalked. Seed pods cylindrical on stalks. It has the distinction of being the first plant genome sequenced as it has a small number of chromosomes, 10, compared to 46 for humans.

Cabbage Family – Brassicaceae

Smith's Pepperwort

Lepidium heterophyllum

An erect to sprawling plant to 50cm, with tiny white flowers, 2-3mm, in clusters with purple anthers. Basal leaves untoothed but those clasping the stem are toothed. Seed pods oval with a notch at tip and a short beak protruding from it. Has been seen in Sark on roadsides, e.g. near Coronation tree, Lt Sark, on way to Derrible and path to the Barracks and other places. Named after Sir James Edward Smith, 1759-1828, a British botanist.

Knotweed Family – Polygonaceae

Knotgrass

Polygonum aviculare

A spreading, hairless annual to 1m from June to November. Very common weed of cultivated ground but not much attention paid to it. Tiny white, pinkish or reddish flowers, 3-6 in clusters in a sheath at base of upper leaf stalks. Leaves on main stem 2-3 times as long as those on the branches but sometimes difficult to distinguish. It gets its name, both common and botanical, from the knotty swellings where the leaves join the stem.

Pink Family – Caryophyllaceae

Common Chickweed

Stellaria media

A very common weed in Sark most of the year in cultivated and waste ground and on roadside verges. Sprawls to 50cm with a row of hairs on alternate sides of the rounded stems. Flowers, 5-9mm, with 5 white petals so deeply notched it looks like more. The 5 downy sepals with pale margins are equal or slightly longer than the petals. Leaves pale green, pointed oval, the lower ones stalked. Can be used in salads.

Pink Family – Caryophyllaceae

Greater Stitchwort

Stellaria holostea

First recorded south of Nat West Bank on roadside bank in 1988 and has been there in this one location only ever since, from April – July, but is common in England. White flowers, 9-11mm, with 5 petals, divided for half their length, and longer than the sepals. Slender stems with narrow lanceolate leaves, unstalked. Its common name is from folklore as it apparently good for easing 'stitches' in the side; a preparation of stitchwort and acorns taken in wine was the standard remedy.

Pink Family – Caryophyllaceae

Common Mouse-ear

Cerastium fontanum

Very common in Sark from spring to November. Erect to sprawling in grassy places, up to 50cm. Flowers 6-10mm, with 5 white, notched petals and 5 sepals of equal length. Lanceolate to oblong leaves, opposite, hairy and unstalked.

Pink Family – Caryophyllaceae

Sticky Mouse-ear

Cerastium glomeratum

Very common in Sark in spring from April onwards. Short annual, to 40cm, very hairy, erect plant with compact white flower clusters, the flowers, 5-8mm, sometimes hardly opening. The 5 petals equal in size to the hairy sepals. Often yellowish-green in colour with ovate leaves opposite on the stem. Seen on bare, disturbed ground, roadsides, and fields.

Pink Family – Caryophyllaceae

Sea Mouse-ear

Cerastium diffusum

Shorter than Common Mouse-ear, to 30cm, found on bare, sandy ground, near the sea. Hairy with flowers, 2-6mm, with usually only 4 notched petals, unlike Common and Sticky Mouse-ears with 5, which are shorter than the sepals. Leaves much smaller than Common Mouse-ear, opposite, unstalked, ovate to oblong. Has been seen along cliff path in Little Sark from silver mines to Duval and quarry at Saut à Juan.

Early morning near the Mill

Pink Family – Caryophyllaceae

Corn Spurrey

Spergula arvensis

A straggly, hairy annual to 40cm with long-stalked, small, white flowers, 4-7mm, and 5 unnotched petals with 5 sepals. Linear greyish leaves in whorls along a very branched, sticky stem. Common in Sark on arable or disturbed ground from April – September. Now considered a weed but in pre- Roman days it was a food crop. Evidence of this from Tollund Man, 400BC, found in a peat bog in Denmark in 1950 whose diet consisted of it among other plants.

Pink Family – Caryophyllaceae

Upright Chickweed

Moenchia erecta

This seems to be a mixture of a plant, not quite a chickweed, nor a stitchwort but within the Caryophyllaceae family. Short and usually erect to 12mm, but hard to see on the sandy ground with small white flowers, 7-9mm with 4 unnotched petals, shorter than the white-edged sepals. Hairless, with stiff, narrow, unstalked leaves. From April to June in sandy, gravely turf. G T Derrick in 1898 said "common on cliffs", but it doesn't appear to be common now. Seen in 2010 near Adonis headland.

Little Sark coastline

Looking east over La Coupée with Bird's-foot trefoil, Thrift and Sea Campion

Pink Family – Caryophyllaceae

Sea Campion

Silene uniflora

Very common in Sark from early spring, on cliffs, rocks and hedgerows but generally near the sea. White flowers 20-25mm, often solitary, 5 notched, spreading petals with inflated calyx tube, pale green with veins, often reddish. Leaves narrow, fleshy, hairless and opposite on stem. White Campion (*Silene latifolia*) and Bladder Campion (*Silene vulgaris*) have not been found on Sark.

Bedstraw Family – Rubiaceae

Cleavers

Galium aparine

Also known as Goose grass as it is a favourite food of geese, but another common name is Sticky Willy, as this straggling plant with curved prickles on its stem can stick to your clothes. Like other bedstraws its leaves are in whorls around the square stem. Common on hedgerows from April.

Bedstraw Family – Rubiaceae

Hedge Bedstraw

Galium album

A scrambling perennial over hedgerows from June with smooth square stems, tiny white 4-petalled flowers, 2-5mm, in clusters, the tips of the petals pointed. Leaves oblong, 1-veined, in whorls of 6-8 on stem, with a bristle-like tip. Fruits wrinkled and hairless. As its name suggests it can be found on hedgerows.

Mill Lane in spring

Bindweed Family – Convolvulaceae

Large Bindweed

Calystegia silvatica

The large funnel-shaped white flowers to 90mm, spread over hedgerows, twining around other plants. Certainly not popular with gardeners and very hard to eradicate because of its rooting system. Can be confused with Hedge Bindweed (*Calystegia sepium*) but it is larger with two inflated bracts which overlap each other and completely cover the sepals. Leaves are arrow-shaped and more pointed.

Nightshade Family – Solanaceae

This Nightshade family is mostly poisonous even though the potato and tomato are members, but they too are poisonous if you eat the wrong part of the plant. There is similarity between the flowers of the potato and tomato and the nightshades.

Black Nighshade

Solanum nigrum ssp. nigrum

Has white flowers with yellow anthers and black berries. It is very common, especially in gardens.

Tall Nightshade

Solanum chenopodioides

Has a specimen near the Power Station. It grows up to 1m, has similar style flowers to Black Nightshade, but with appressed hairs on the stem, and more purplish-black fruits. (not illustrated).

Potato flower

Primrose Family – Primulaceae

Brookweed

Samolus valerandi

A plant of the Primrose Family, delicate and straggly, found in damp places especially near the sea. It was first seen by G T Derrick in 1897 at Fontaines, Little Sark and can still be seen there today. Other places where it has been seen are near the steps to Dixcart beach and at L'Eperquerie from June onwards. 5-petalled tiny, white flowers, 2-4mm, on long stalks with a tiny bract about halfway. Leaves oval, some almost spoon-shaped, untoothed, mainly in basal rosette. Globular fruits.

Daisy Family – Asteraceae

There are several types of cudweed in Sark with the Cape Cudweed the most common and most conspicuous. All are covered in whitish down. 'Gnaphalium' comes from Greek for wool or English 'cudweed' or 'cotton weed' which refers to its cottony hairs.

Cape Cudweed

Gnaphalium undulatum

Grows up to 60 cm, has tiny yellowy-white flowers in clusters with woolly white bracts beneath. Leaves narrow, lanceolate, woolly underneath, and clasping the stem. Seen on coastal walks. Originally from South Africa but has spread throughout the island, probably extended from NW France to Channel Islands as it is less apparent on mainland U.K. First recorded in Sark in 1902 by CP Hurst.

Cape Cudweed growing with Marsh Cudweed

Daisy Family – Asteraceae

Other Cudweeds in Sark are:

Marsh Cudweed

Gnaphalium uliginosum

Found on disturbed ground and tracks to 25cm, also common but less noticeable with yellow/brownish flowers in clusters at top of stem. Narrow, lanceolate, woolly leaves clasping the stem, with some overtopping flower heads.

Narrow-leaved Cudweed

Filago gallica

Very rare, and found in Sark only and not the other Channel Islands.

Common Cudweed

Filago vulgaris

Grows to 20cm. Only seen occasionally on rough ground.

Daisy Family – Asteraceae

Yarrow

Achillea millefolium

This downy, medium sized perennial to 80cm has many small flowerheads, 4-6mm, comprising of creamy/yellow disc florets surrounded by white, sometimes tinged pink, ray florets in umbel-like clusters. Leaves dark green, feathery and very divided, hence the Latin name millefolium, meaning 'thousand leaves'. Legend has it that Achilles used it to heal wounds. Can be found in grassy places and is fairly common.

Making hay

Daisy Family – Asteraceae

Chamomile

Chamaemelum nobile

There are various types of Chamomile and Mayweed which look similar and can be very confusing, but I will only discuss Chamomile, which is usually found on short grass. Low-growing, hairy and spreading perennial to 30cm, with daisy-like flowers, 18-25mm, the scent often attracting one's attention in short grass. Solitary flowers, the white rayed-florets turn down on old flowerheads. Flower bracts downy, with whitish margins. Leaves feathery, very divided. Chamomile tea is not made from this plant but from Scented Mayweed (*Matricaria chamomilla*), (not illustrated), which is hairless, with greenish/white bracts, but has similar flowers and is also aromatic.

Daisy Family – Asteraceae

Oxeye Daisy

Leucanthemum vulgare

Like a large daisy which appears on hedgerows and other grassy areas with a golden centre of yellow disc-florets surrounded by white rayed-florets, solitary, 25-60mm. Dark green leaves with upper leaves narrower than lower ones, deeply toothed, and clasping the stem. Basal leaves stalked. The garden Marguerite is a related species. Very common in Sark from May onwards.

Giant Butterbur on Harbour Hill pedestrian path

Daisy Family – Asteraceae

Giant Butterbur

Petasites japonicus

The large cauliflower-like creamy flowerheads appear before the leaves from late January. Leaves can be up to 1 metre across and can grow to 1.5 metres tall, rhubarb like, toothed, green above and downy beneath. Tradition has it that the large leaves were used to wrap butter, hence its name. It used to be planted in Victorian gardens. A male clone was introduced from the Mediterranean in 1806 to UK and naturalised in 1835. In Sark it was first noted by Dr RM Veall in a damp area of Harbour Hill pedestrian path in 1992 and has flourished since then.

Carrot Family – Apiaceae

Hogweed

Heracleum sphondylium

Very common, if not too common, in Sark on roadsides from May with stout, coarse, hairy, hollow stems up to 3m. Off-white flowers with unequal sized petals in umbels with many rays, about 20cm across, and only a few bracts. Leaves pinnate, broad and hairy. Can be harmful to sensitive skin. Sark does not have Giant Hogweed (*Heracleum mantegazzianum*).

Left: Wild Carrot leaf

Right: Hogweed leaf

Hogweed with Red Campion near Dos d'Ane

Carrot Family – Apiaceae

Wild Carrot

Daucus carota ssp. carota

Another member of the umbellifer family, frequent in Sark during the summer months on roadsides, cliff paths and fields. Solid hairy stems up to 1.5m with 3 forked bracts under the compound flower head. The umbels begin red, then turn white and finally turn into a brown concave fruiting head, known as a 'bird's nest'. Sometimes the white flowerheads have a red centre and one has been found on the path to Derrible Bay with a yellow centre. Leaves feathery and very divided, 3-pinnate. Ancestor of the garden carrot, but the wild carrot's roots are totally inedible. The Sea Carrot (*ssp. gummifer*) is almost inseparable in Sark from *ssp. carota*.

Wild Carrot at La Coupée

Waterfall above Port du Moulin

Carrot Family – Apiaceae

Hemlock Water-dropwort

Oenanthe crocata

A very poisonous hairless perennial found in damp areas. Grows to 2.5m with thick, ridged, hollow stems. White flowers in umbels, 5-10cm across, rayed with some linear bracts. Leaves glossy, pinnately divided with leaflets not unlike celery. Fruits cylindrical with long styles. Found in Dixcart Valley, Creux Belet, Vallon D'Or and other damp spots. Very invasive.

Orchid Family – Orchidaceae

Autumn Lady's-tresses

Spiranthes spiralis

The short erect spike, 3-12 cm, has its 7-20 small flowers arranged spirally on the stem. Blue-green leaves form a rosette at the base. In Sark it can be found in short grass especially lawns and the old graveyard by Methodist Church from late July.

Onion Family – Alliaceae

Three-cornered Garlic

Allium triquetrum

Some people think it is a white bluebell, including me when I came to live in Sark first. Stems triangular, flowers white and bell-shaped, drooping on stalks, with a narrow green stripe down the centre of each petal. A garlic type smell pervades the air when near them, hence also known as Stinking Onions. Originally from the Mediterranean but first recorded in Sark in 1896. Since then it has spread considerably and is very common in spring, in valleys and along roadsides. Also known as Three-cornered Leek.

Different from Ramsons (*Allium ursinum*), which does not grow on Sark, which has flowerheads in clusters at the top of a long stem with large, broad leaves.

Poppy Family – Papaveraceae

Common Ramping-fumitory

Fumaria muralis ssp. boraei

This scrambling weed over hedgerows and on disturbed ground is common in Sark. Spikes of pinkish tube-like flowers tipped with purple with up to 20 flowers in each spike. Slender leaves, deeply divided with very tangled stems. Seen April to October.

Stonecrop Family – Crassulaceae

Mossy Stonecrop

Crassula tillaea

There are 4 plants from the Stonecrop family in Sark, the one which appears in April and May is the Mossy Stonecrop, a bright red, creeping annual, almost like moss. The tiny white flowers, 1-2mm, are solitary on very thin stems with crowded leaves. Seen over by Pilcher Monument and other coastal areas.

Stonecrop Family – Crassulaceae

English Stonecrop

Sedum anglicum

It appears before the Mossy stonecrop disappears, from June onwards. It is mat-forming with white (tinged pink) flowers, 11-12mm, larger than the Mossy Stonecrop. Leaves fleshy, hair-less, clasping the stem. Found on rocks, cliffs and roadsides and is very common.

Navelwort and English Stonecrop

Pea Family – Fabaceae

Common Vetch

Vicia sativa

This species is complicated as it was originally thought to be represented by 2 species, *Vicia sativa* and *Vicia angustifolia* (Narrow-leaved Vetch). However *V. angustifolia* is now regarded as a subspecies of *V. sativa*, called *ssp. nigra*. There are two other subspecies of *V. sativa*, ssp. *segetalis* and *ssp. sativa*. But for general recognition the following is a basic description. Sprawling or scrambling in grassy places with reddish-purple pea like flowers, singly or in pairs. Leaves 3-5 pairs of leaflets and branched tendrils. Fairly common in fields and grassy places.

Pea Family – Fabaceae

Common Restharrow

Ononis repens

A short to medium sprawling shrub with tough hairy stems. Pink flowers, usually single, 12-20mm with the side petals (wings) usually as long as the joined lower petals (keel). Leaves of 3 leaflets, small and toothed. Got its common name from the days before tractors when farmers ploughing or harrowing their fields used to be slowed down by the matted stems and deep roots of this plant. In Sark it has been seen along La Coupée and on the steps down to Grand Grève, now no longer in use, and on cliff path between Venus Pool area and Port Gorey in July-August.

La Moserie cottage, Little Sark

Pea Family – Fabaceae

Red Clover

Trifolium pratense

Common sprawling, downy perennial with pink-purple, egg-shaped, flowerheads, 12-15mm. Oval leaflets, toothed, with a whitish crescent-shaped mark on each leaf. Stipules triangular and pointed. May-Nov in grassland and roadsides. Good for enriching the soil or as animal fodder and bees, butterflies and moths love it.

Crane's-bill Family – Geraniaceae

Dove's-foot Crane's-bill

Geranium molle

There are several Crane's-bills on Sark, the most common being Dove's-foot Crane's-bill. A low/short erect, to sprawling, hairy annual which grows to about 40cm and is found in fields and grassy banks. Flowers pink to purple, 6-10mm, with the 5 petals all notched, in pairs on long stalks. Leaves roundish, hairy with 7-9 lobes, cut to at least half way. Fruits hairless.

Left: Dove's-foot Crane's-bill

Right: Cut-leaved Crane's-bill

Crane's-bill Family – Geraniaceae

Cut-leaved Crane's-bill

Geranium dissectum

Pink-purple flowers, 8-10mm, with notched petals and sepals with a bristle. Leaves very divided. Fruits downy. On cultivated and waste ground. Specimen in photo near La Moserie.

Round-leaved Crane's-bill

Geranium rotundifolium

Flowers pink, with barely notched petals and rounded leaves, mostly 5-lobed. Seen near Nat West Bank.

Pencilled Crane's-bill

Geranium versicolor

Has distinctive white or pale lilac flowers with purple veins on petals. Originally from mountain woods in Eastern Mediterranean, but probably came to Sark as a garden plant. First seen in Sark by G T Derrick in 1896 in Dixcart Lane. Now some specimens near Beauvoir and also Rue du Fort on roadside bank.

Crane's-bill Family – Geraniaceae

Common Stork's-bill

Erodium cicutarium

Also from the Crane's-bill Family and very common in Sark from April onwards, especially near the coast. Leaves of the stork's-bill are pinnate and never lobed like the crane's-bill. A short, sprawling, sometimes erect annual with pink-purple flowers, sometimes white, and sometimes with a blackish spot at the base of the two upper petals. Fruits are fascinating with long beaks which split into five segments when ripe, then twist into a corkscrew shape with the seed attached. The seed, with the help of this corkscrew, burrows into the ground. (see photo on opposite page).

Crane's-bill Family – Geraniaceae

Musk Stork's-bill

Erodium moschatum
A very hairy annual with pinnate, oval and toothed leaves. Flowers purple, 16-24mm, in clusters of 5-12. Only seen occasionally on Sark but recently near La Fregondée, old Grand Beauregard Hotel site and also on the way to Gouliot Headland.

Fruit of Stork's-bill

View towards Guernsey from Little Sark

Willowherb Family – Onagraceae

There are several willowherbs found in Sark but most are occasional. All have pink flowers with four notched petals and undivided leaves, but the shape of the leaf is important as is the shape of the stigma, either club-shaped or divided into four lobes. The seed-pods are long, four sided, and when they split open they reveal a wonderful cottony hairy structure with the seeds attached.

American Willowherb (*Epilobium ciliatum*) reddish stems, club shaped stigma, has been seen in Harbour Hill quarry. **Hoary Willowherb** (*Epilobium parviflorum*) with 4 lobed stigma, prefers damp areas, like Creux Belet, and also Harbour Hill quarry. **Great Willowherb** (*Epilobium hirsutum*), the largest flowered and tallest to nearly 2m, seen Harbour Hill path, and at Vallon d'Or. **Broad-leaved Willowherb** (*Epilobium montanum*), outside Stocks Hotel and in La Seigneurie garden. **Square-stalked Willowherb** (*Epilobium tetragonum*) by rough ground at Le Vallon d'Or, and Dixcart Hotel garden. **Short-fruited Willowherb** (*Epilobium obscurum*) on paving at the Barracks.

Fruit of Willowherb

Mallow Family – Malvaceae

Common Mallow

Malva sylvestris

Common from June onwards on roadside banks, bare ground and in fields. Upright, but sprawls to about 1m. The 5 notched petalled pink flowers, up to 4cm, have dark veins, the sepal ring joins at the base only. Leaves are palmate, lobed and veined. Fruit is rounded and flat and resembles a little cheese, hence sometimes known as cheesecake or cheese flower.

Mallow Family – Malvaceae

Tree-mallow

Malva arborea

A much larger plant than Common Mallow (*Malva sylvestris*). Woody, tall to 3m, pinkish-purple flowers with distinct dark veins and dark centre. Found on coasts. Specimens seen on rocks near Rouge Terrier, at La Rondellerie and near Les Lâches.

Thrift near Venus Pool headland, Little Sark

Thrift Family – Plumbaginaceae

Thrift

Armeria maritima

A very common site on cliff tops and rocks throughout Sark from April onwards. Has great capacity to endure harsh environments because of its long roots. Grows in tufts with round, tight heads of small pink flowers above papery bracts on leafless stems. Leaves linear and fleshy, tufted at the base. Also known as Sea Pink. It used to appear on the reverse side of the pre-decimalization 3d coin.

Knotweed Family – Polygonaceae

Sheep's Sorrel

Rumex acetosella

Can be seen from April as a red hue on grassy places, (photo taken on common towards Venus Pool). Smaller and more slender than Common Sorrel to not more than 30cm in height. The flower spike is fairly open unlike the Common Sorrel which is more compact. Leaves are linear to oblong-lanceolate with narrow forward or sideways pointing basal lobes. Fruits with no wart.

Knotweed Family – Polygonaceae

Common Sorrel

Rumex acetosa

This sorrel can be seen from late April. Much taller than Sheep's Sorrel, up to 80cm, on roadsides and grassland. Flowers reddish, compact, in terminal spikes. Leaves more arrow-shaped with the basal lobes turning backwards and the top leaves unstalked, clasping the stem. Fruits round with a small wart. A sour tasting plant used in Tudor times instead of lemons. Also used to remove ink or iron stains from linen; I must confess I haven't tried it.

Pink Family – Caryophyllaceae

Rock Sea-spurrey

Spergularia rupicola

Common in Sark on cliffs, rocks and walls near the sea. Sprawling stems with a sometimes woody base. Flowers with 5 pink petals and 5 sepals of equal size, 8-10mm, with yellow anthers. Leaves narrow and fleshy with a sharp tip. April to September. Can be seen on east side of path descending towards La Coupée and other coastal areas.

Pink Family – Caryophyllaceae

Sand Spurrey

Spergularia rubra

This spurrey grows inland, sprawling to about 25cm. Found on tracks, (specimen in photo just outside the Barracks), and sandy or gravely places. Fairly common in Sark with pale pink flowers, 3-5mm, 5 petals and 5 sepals. Greyish whorled leaves, always ending in a tiny bristle. Usually smaller than Rock Sea-spurrey, also flowers a bit later from May to September.

Pink Family – Caryophyllaceae

Red Campion

Silene dioica

Very common in Sark from March to November in woods, on hedgerows, on roadsides, up to 1m tall. Flowers various shades of pink to red with 5 notched petals. Stems downy with ovate, hairy, stalked leaves in opposite pairs, the upper leaves stalkless (sessile). 'Dioicus' means having male and female plants, therefore two plants are needed to produce seed.

Mill Lane with Red Campion

Primrose Family – Primulaceae

Scarlet Pimpernel

Anagallis arvensis ssp. arvensis

A sprawling little plant with vivid red flowers, 10-15mm, on long slender stalks appearing only in the sun. Known long ago as 'poor man's weather glass'. The centre has a reddish-purple eye with 5 stamens. Leaves sessile, pointed oval, opposite and paired. Found in fields, roadsides, on lawns and disturbed ground. Four other colour forms have been found in Sark. *Vinacea* (wine), noted by the Lighthouse signpost, at the base of a wall,

near La Valette in 2005 but has since been strimmed. *Azurea* (blue), seen recently in the garden of Clos Gorey, Little Sark. Seen also some years ago in the field south of the Barracks. *Pallida* (white), seen in 2009 in field north near La Grand Creux. *Carnea* (pink), seen at La Rondellerie on waste ground by building site in 2007. There is a Blue Pimpernel (*Anagallis arvensis ssp. foemina*) which has not been found on Sark.

Scarlet Pimpernel with Field Bindweed, Common Bird's-foot Trefoil and Germander Speedwell on short grass

Bindweed Family – Convolvulaceae

Field Bindweed

Convolvulus arvensis

Field Bindweed has long stalked single white or pink and white flowers to 25mm from leaf axils, with a pair of bracteoles on the stalks below the flowers. Leaves long stalked and arrow-shaped.   Found sprawling on cultivated or waste ground and roadsides and is very common.

Bedstraw Family – Rubiaceae

Field Madder

Sherardia arvensis

Can be seen on arable land and grassy places. It has tiny pale pink flowers with four petals in clusters surrounded by leaf bracts. Hairy, square stems, and leaves in whorls. A good patch has been seen on the cliff path from silver mines heading west from April, also the field south of the Barracks in Little Sark and in several other places too.

Heather Family – Ericaceae

Bell Heather

Erica cinerea and

Heather (Ling)

Calluna vulgaris

Both of these heathers are plentiful from July onwards. They give a wonderful purple hue to the landscape looking towards Pilcher Monument from Little Sark, on Eperquerie Common and the odd clumps near the sea.

Difference between the two is that Ling has paler flowers in spikes, linear leaves in opposite rows along a slender stem, whereas Bell Heather has darker, more purple, bell-shaped flowers clustered near top, with needle-like dark green leaves in whorls of 3 with clusters of smaller leaves at the base of each whorl. Cross-leaved Heath (*Erica tetralix*) frequent in British Isles is not found in Sark.

Note: Photos of Ling see page 132

Relaxing by Pilcher Monument

Heather Family – Ericaceae

Heather (Ling)

Calluna vulgaris

Description page 130

Ling and Bell Heather growing together

Left: Heather (Ling)

Right: Bell Heather

Looking north towards Les Autelets

Gentian Family – Gentianaceae

Common Centaury

Centaurium erythraea

Only one member of the gentian family is in Sark, the Common Centaury, and it is fairly common from late June onwards on roadsides and on cliff paths. A short annual to 50cm, but generally much smaller, with clear pink flowers in upright clusters. Leaves pointed, oval and opposite. Got its name from centaur Chiron of Greek mythology who is said to have cured himself of a wound with this plant inflicted by Hydra. Besides wounds it is also claimed to cure freckles!

Speedwell Family – Veronicaceae

Foxglove

Digitalis purpurea

These familiar, upright, stately, pink-purple flowers in long unbranched spikes can have up to 80 bell-shaped flowers on a single stem. Leaves large and downy, the lowest in a basal rosette. Very common in Sark from June onwards. Known as Fairy Bells in some places. Poisonous, although a compound extracted from its leaves is used for heart problems. First written description of a plant on Sark was a white variety of this recorded by Thomas Knowlton on a visit in 1726.

Speedwell Family – Veronicaceae

Weasel's-snout

Misopates orontium

Also known as Lesser Snapdragon. Grows up to 50cm with distinctive single pink-purple flowers, 10-15mm, with rounded pouch, in axils of upper leaves which are linear. Can be seen from July in arable fields or sometimes as a garden weed. Fairly common.

A lone Weasel's-snout in arable field

Dead-nettle Family – Lamiaceae

There are several plants on Sark from the Dead-nettle Family. They have very distinctive flowerheads with 2-lipped lower petals, an open mouth, and then a type of hood on top. The flowers are found in whorls up the leafy stem of the plant. Stems usually quadrangular.

Field Woundwort

Stachys arvensis

Can be found in vegetable patches, in hedgerows and fields. A hairy, usually erect plant to 25cm, with dull pink-purple flowers, 6-7mm, and long sepal teeth. Leaves are oval, almost heart-shaped, and bluntly toothed, with the upper leaves unstalked (sessile). Woundwort has been used to treat wounds since the ancient Greeks as it has antiseptic qualities, apparently. Seen April to October.

Dead-nettle Family – Lamiaceae

Marsh Woundwort

Stachys palustris

Since 1983 this plant has been recorded only on Rue Lucas, across from the telephone exchange from June to October. Grows up to 1m with pink-purple flowers in spikes. Leaves oval, toothed, opposite up the quadrangular stem. The ground must be fairly damp in order for it to survive.

Dead-nettle Family – Lamiaceae

Hedge Woundwort

Stachys sylvatica

Grows to 1m, hairy, red/purple flowers, 12-18mm long, with white markings. Leaves heart-shaped, toothed and stalked on square stems. Seen on Harbour Hill pedestrian path and occasionally other shady places, from June to September.

Dead-nettle Family – Lamiaceae

Henbit Dead-nettle

Lamium amplexicaule

This is another 'hooded' little plant in the Dead-nettle family to 25cm. The flowers are more pinkish-purple usually appearing above the cluster of stalkless, toothed leaves, with lower leaves stalked. Found on cultivated and disturbed ground from March onwards.

Wild Thyme and Sheep's-bit growing on côtil near L'Etac

Dead-nettle Family – Lamiaceae

Wild Thyme

Thymus polytrichus

Mat-forming, woody, low growing plant to 10cm, on dry grassland, heaths and especially by cliffs in Sark, e.g. Pilcher Monument, Hog's Back, Gouliot Headland etc. The tiny pinkish-purple flowers are slightly aromatic in dense terminal heads. Leaves evergreen, oval, opposite.

Lousewort in old graveyard

Broomrape Family – Orobanchaceae

Lousewort

Pedicularis sylvatica

A short, spreading perennial with pink-purple flowers in leafy spikes. The flowerhead shaped like a hood with a 3-lobed spreading lower lip. The name derives from old belief that the plant infected sheep with lice but this is unproven, however, the name sticks. Found on heaths and damp fields. In Sark it can be found on the heath opposite Vermandaye, Little Sark, and in old graveyard by Methodist Church, Creux Belet as well as other areas.

Broomrape Family – Orobanchaceae

Ivy Broomrape

Orobanche hederae

Broomrapes are parasites on the roots of other plants. They have no green pigment so live off the host plant. This, at times, is difficult to identify as the broomrape might not be beside the plant but at a certain distance. Ivy Broomrape is the most common in Sark because its host is Atlantic Ivy (*Hedera hibernica*). It occurs in spikes of cream flowers with purple veins on stems to 60cm with brown scales. Broomrapes do not have leaves. Has been seen from May onwards on path to Le Pot, near the old mining smelter towards Port Gorey, on Harbour Hill and other places.

Little Sark windmill

Daisy Family – Asteraceae

Common Knapweed

Centaurea nigra

A medium height plant to 1m, with stiff, ridged, hairy stems. The swollen base of the reddish-pink flowerhead is covered in bracts with dark brown fringed attachments. Upper leaves narrow, unstalked and alternate. Leaves at base with shallow teeth. Fairly common in grassy places from June onwards. Specimen in photo seen along Rue de la Coupée before Dixcart Lane.

Daisy Family – Asteraceae

Winter Heliotrope

Petasites fragrans

The lilac coloured flowerheads on spikes appear from November through to early spring. The rounded leaves are much smaller than Butterbur (page 93), 10-20cm across. Usually found along roadsides, Mill Lane and Dixcart Lane, for instance.

Daisy Family – Asteraceae

Hemp-agrimony

Eupatorium cannabinum

A tall perennial to 1.5m with reddish, hairy stems found in damp areas, e.g. Creux Belet, pedestrian path up Harbour Hill, Fontaines Bay, Lt Sark. Pinkish-mauve flowerheads in clusters at top of stems surrounded by a ring of purple tipped bracts. Each flowerhead has 5 or 6 florets with long white styles. Palmate leaves in 3 sections, with toothed edges. Flowers in late summer.

Hemp -agrimony with Jersey Tiger Moth and Wall Brown butterfly

Red Valerian on wall of Clos à Jaon

Valerian Family – Valerianaceae

Red Valerian

Centranthus ruber

This is a fairly tall, usually unbranched, perennial with red-pink flowers in loose rounded clusters. Leaves oval and pointed, the upper leaves sessile (stalkless). Butterflies and day flying moths love it, so it is to be encouraged! Can be seen on top of the wall at La Ville Roussel and Clos à Jaon from late April onwards. Also found in quarries, but one of the most common places is on walls. First recorded in Sark in 1901 by GT Derrick 'Post Office to La Ville. On garden wall'.

Arum Family – Araceae

Lords and Ladies

Arum maculatum

These flowers have a purple spadix (or 'stem'), surrounded by a yellow-green hooded spathe, (leaf like structure) seen in spring. Leaves arrow-shaped, green, including the veins, some with dark spots. Bright orange-red berries on spikes in autumn and very poisonous. Found in shady places usually.

Orchid Family – Orchidaceae

Heath Spotted-orchid

Dactylorhiza maculata

Flower spike is thick with flowers from pale pink to pale purple with small blotches of red-purple. Leaves are fairly narrow with black spots. Found at Creux Belet in the wet valley from early June, also at Vallon D'Or.

Early-purple Orchid

Orchis mascula

Just recently re-discovered after many years, but in a different spot, down lane east of the mill near L'Etoile, in March 2009 and in Le Manoir garden 2010. Purple flowers and glossy leaves with dark spots, in basal rosette.

Tufted Vetch with Hotel Petit Champ in distance

Pea Family – Fabaceae

Tufted Vetch

Vicia cracca

A scrambling plant over hedges and through grass with its blue-purple flowers, 8-12mm, in spikes of up to 30 flowers. Leaves with 6-12 pairs of leaflets, ending with branched tendrils. June-August. In Sark has been seen recently on the road to La Coupée between Sue's Guille's tea garden and Dixcart Lane, but not in 2009. In 2007 a large patch was seen at the end of the lane just south of La Vaurocque on the west side of La Rue de la Coupée.

Milkwort Family – Polygalaceae

Common Milkwort

Polygala vulgaris

This very attractive little plant to 30cm can vary in colour form, usually blue but can be white, pink or a wonderfully rich mauve. Many short-stalked unusual flowers of 3 green outer sepals, 2 larger blue/pink inner sepals almost concealing a tube of petals fused with stamens, grouped at the tip of the stem. Simple, pointed, lanceolate leaves are alternatively up the stem. Specimens in photos on the way to Le Pot. Can also be seen Harbour Hill pedestrian path.

Heath Milkwort

Polygala serpyllifolia

Differs from Common Milkwort in that the leaves at base are opposite each other. Also usually more than 10 flowers together whereas Common Milkwort has usually less than 10. A white specimen has been seen on heath opposite Vermandaye in Little Sark but can be blue or pink too. (not illustrated)

Violet Family – Violaceae

Common Dog-violet

Viola riviniana

The very abundant pretty blue-violet flower can be seen from March onwards. Different from Sweet Violet (*Viola odorata*) which may have escaped from gardens, in being unscented, in having pointed sepals, paler spurs and only slightly downy leaves and stalks. Leaves heart-shaped and long stalked. The word 'dog' given to wild flowers indicates inferiority; perhaps it is because it does not have a nice scent like *Viola odorata*.

Rock Sea-lavender near Derrible Bay

Thrift Family – Plumbaginaceae

Rock Sea-lavender

Limonium binervosum ssp. sarniense

There are two varieties of *ssp. sarniense* in Sark, one called *sarniense*, which has only been found at Port Gorey, on a path not now in use, and in the other Channel Islands. The other variety *sercquense*, occurs in other areas in Sark, Rouge Terrier, Derrible Bay and near Venus Pool. Both are found on cliff paths from July. Var. *sarniense* is taller to 50cm and more erect, whereas var. *sercquense* is much smaller up to 30cm. Both are branched, with small blue and white flowers clustered on spikes towards the top of the stem. Leaves narrow, fleshy, forming at the base. Sark is the only place in the world where var. *sercquense* is found.

Flax Family – Linaceae

Pale Flax

Linum bienne

The wonderfully pale delicate blue to lilac flower can be found in the old graveyard, and other fields on Sark. It grows up to 60cm on a long, narrow, but wiry stem with linear leaves. The 5 petals have darker veins and can drop easily. Only appears in sunshine and can close early in the afternoon after the midday sun which makes it more difficult to find. Has been seen in old graveyard, near La Gentière and near Le Vieux Port.

Periwinkle Family – Apocynaceae

Lesser Periwinkle

Vinca minor and

Greater Periwinkle

Vinca major

These are trailing plants found on hedge-rows and in woods, but not so frequent in Sark. Both have blue-violet, solitary flowers with 5 petals, but Greater Periwinkle has slightly larger flowers to 50mm, broader lan-ceolate leaves with longer stalks, and stems which root at the tips. Lesser Periwinkle has flowers up to 30mm, sepals more pointed and hairless with narrower leaves and stems which root at leaf nodes. Greater Periwinkle was first recorded in Sark by GT Derrick in 1896 at 'Epercurie, Saignie cliffs' but more recently seen in Mill Lane and on the way to Fregondée.

Borage Family – Boraginaceae

Giant Viper's-bugloss

Echium pininana

Originally from the Canary Islands as a garden plant but has established itself well outside of gardens in Sark. A biennial with leaves only in the first year before a splendid, immensely tall, leafy spike with small blue flowers appears in the second year. The impressive row of 'soldiers' in the photo was seen in Little Sark but the exotic-looking plant appears in many places now. Also known as Giant Echium.

Giant Viper's-bugloss, silver mine area, Little Sark

Near path to Grève de la Ville

Borage Family – Boraginaceae

Bugloss

Anchusa arvensis

A hairy annual from the same family as forget-me-nots. It grows in arable fields and has tiny blue flowers, 4-6mm, the blue suddenly attracting one's attention. The centre of the flowers are white, are almost stalkless, and grow in clusters at the top of the leafy stem which can be up to 50cm. Leaves are lanceolate, wavy and covered with hairs. Anchusa in Greek means paint as a reddish extract from its roots was used to stain wood.

Borage Family – Boraginaceae

The story about forget-me-nots is rather poignant. One day in Medieval times a knight and his lady were strolling along a river bank when the knight bent to pick a bunch of flowers for his lady. Unfortunately his armour, weighing too much, overbalanced him and he fell into the river. As he was drowning he threw the bunch of flowers to his beloved lady and shouted 'forget-me-not'!

Early Forget-me-not

Myosotis ramosissima

As the name implies this is the earliest forget-me-not to appear in the spring. It is so tiny it is easy to overlook it, but a sudden dash of blue on the ground makes one realise there is something there. On closer examination this low, sprawling plant with flowers only 1-3mm, a pin head size, with a yellow centre, in little clusters is at your feet. The hairy lower leaves form a rosette. It can be found in bare rocky places and in dry soils.

Borage Family – Boraginaceae

Changing Forget-me-not

Myosotis discolor

Another forget-me-not not easily seen, but once you get a trained eye a sudden blue/grey haze colour in the grass can attract your attention. Then you notice a small plant like a shepherd's crook, usually no more than a few inches tall on the grass. As the flowers open the 'crook' unfurls and the tiny flowers change from white to yellow, sometimes pink to blue – a truly delightful sight. The lower, hairy leaves form a rosette.

Creux Belet

Borage Family – Boraginaceae

There are other forget-me-nots in Sark but the Early and the Changing Forget-me-nots (pages 168 and 169 respectively) are the most common and can be seen from April and May. The **Creeping forget-me-not** (*Myosotis secunda*) so far seems to be found only in the damp area of Creux Belet from June. It sprawls out through the damp grass with stem hairs appressed (flattened) above but spreading below.

The garden Forget-me-not, a variety of the Field Forget-me-not (*Myosotis arvensis*), is sometimes seen as a garden escape, (not illustrated).

Nightshade Family – Solanaceae

Bittersweet

Solanum dulcamara

A very colourful sprawling perennial with bright purple flowers and yellow anthers. Its fruit changes colour from green, to yellow and finally to red and are poisonous. Also known as Woody Nightshade. Can be found in a variety of areas in Sark, by roadsides, on cliff paths etc. from June onwards. The potato and tomato are from the same family and have similar flowers.

Potato flower

Speedwell Family – Veronicaceae

Ivy-leaved Toadflax

Cymbalaria muralis

A trailing, hairless plant on walls, with lilac coloured flowers and a yellow honey guide which attracts bees. After the flowers have been fertilized the stalks curl around and push the capsules into cracks in the wall. Some released seeds remain to germinate and give a continuous spread of wall cover. Common in Sark especially by the Collinette, La Seigneurie garden, and on the wall of Rose Cottage from spring onwards. Introduced to gardens from central and southern Europe end of 16th century, but spread to the wild even though difficult to germinate. First seen in Sark in 1892 by WF Miller.

Speedwell Family – Veronicaceae

Germander Speedwell

Veronica chamaedrys

There are many different speedwells on Sark but one of the most common is Germander Speedwell with bright azure blue flowers with a white eye, 10mm across, on short stalks. Hairy and sprawling with two opposite lines of hairs down the stem. Leaves opposite on stem, hairy, pointed, oval and toothed. Can be seen in grassy places from late April.

Speedwell Family – Veronicaceae

Thyme-leaved Speedwell

Veronica serpyllifolia

As its name suggests the leaves are small, oval, untoothed and not unlike thyme leaves. A low, creeping and rooting plant with pale blue or white flowers with dark veins, 5-10mm, on short stalks. Nice specimen recently on wall opposite La Seigneurie gardens.

Speedwell Family – Veronicaceae

Wall speedwell

Veronica arvensis

A hairy perennial with tiny blue flowers, 2-3mm, hardly noticeable, and drop easily, partly hidden by untoothed leaf-like bracts. Leaves alternate, oval, and toothed. Found on dry, bare places. Specimen in photo on gravel.

Common Field-speedwell

Veronica persica

A single long-stalked bright blue flower, with lowest petal palest, at base of upper leaves. Leaves oval to triangular, alternate on stem except for lowest ones which are toothed and short stalked. Was originally from SW Asia but arrived in UK with agricultural seed. In Sark it was first recorded 'Plentiful in the churchyard' by WF Miller in 1892. This specimen is by the roadside near Coronation tree, Little Sark.

Speedwell Family – Veronicaceae

Ivy-leaved Speedwell

Veronica hederifolia

A low spreading hairy annual found on bare or disturbed ground. As the name suggests the leaves are similar in shape to those of ivy. Solitary pale blue or lilac flowers on slender stalks from leaf axils.

Heath Speedwell

Veronica officinalis

A hairy perennial with small lilac flowers with darker veins in spikes. Leaves oval, toothed, hairy, with very short stalks. This specimen found on heath opposite Vermandaye in Little Sark.

Dead-Nettle Family – Lamiaceae

Ground-ivy

Glechoma hederacea

Common in fields and is a low, creeping plant to 30cm, with blue-violet flowers and leaves not ivy-shaped at all but more kidney-shaped, toothed and long-stalked. Apparently until hops were introduced into England in 16th century Ground-ivy leaves were added instead to ale during brewing to clear the liquid and sharpen the flavour. Another use of the leaves in olden days was to infuse them in boiling water to alleviate sore throats. I must admit I have never tried it.

Dead-Nettle Family – Lamiaceae

Selfheal

Prunella vulgaris

Many people get annoyed when this appears in lawns; I suppose I would too except my lawn is really just grass with lots of tiny flowers appearing in it before it is mown from time to time. This plant has a terminal spike of blue-violet colour flowers, up to 30cm, with the upper petal hooded. Leaves pointed oval, slightly toothed. With a name like selfheal, it surely must have had great healing qualities. Apparently it was used to heal wounds, and a syrup was made from it for internal injuries in medieval times. Common in grassy places.

Variety of wild flowers, roadside, Little Sark (including Sheep's-bit, Lady's Bedstraw, Red Campion and Wild Carrot)

Bellflower Family – Campanulaceae

Sheep's-bit

Jasione montana

This plant can get mixed up with Scabious but it belongs to the Bellflower family and is seen much earlier in the season, from May. Also known as Blue bonnets or Blue buttons because of the bright blue rounded flowerheads, 20-35mm. Leaves in a spiral pattern around the slender stem, linear to oblong with wavy edges. Common on cliffs, roadsides and heath and is sometimes cropped by sheep, hence the name 'bit' by sheep.

Valerian Family – Valerianaceae

Keel-fruited Cornsalad

Valerianella carinata

The most common in Sark, also known as Lamb's lettuce, possibly because it appeared at lambing time or that lambs liked it, but it was originally grown in England for winter salad as the leaves are meant to be rich in vitamins and minerals. Grows to 15cm with tiny lilac flowers in a rounded cluster, often at the fork of very branched stems. Oblong leaves, rounded at the top, opposite on the stem. The main difference between this and Common Cornsalad (*Valerianella locusta*) is the fruit, as it is keeled rather than grooved. Seen in hedgerows and on roadsides from April.

Teasel Family – Dipsacaceae

Wild Teasel

Dipsacus fullonum

A very conspicuous plant to 2m, with very prickly stems. Conical or egg-shaped pink-purple flowerheads. Leaves also prickly. Found on a variety of habitats, usually damp. Specimen in photo taken on path to Grand Grève, now no longer in use. Also seen at Derrible and Harbour Hill path, July –August.

Iris Family – Iridaceae

Stinking Iris

Iris foetidissima

A tufted plant up to 80cm, with flowers at top of a spike composed of purple outer tepals, (when petals and sepals are similar to each other), and yellow inner tepals. Leaves dark green, long, linear and flat. When leaf crushed it gives a smell of burnt milk or roast beef, but not everyone is offended by it. When seed capsule splits it reveals bright orange seeds in autumn with flowers from April. Found mostly in shaded places.

Iris Family – Iridaceae

Sand Crocus

Romulea columnae

This very special tiny flower, 10-12mm, appears in April-May, for a short time. It has six pointed mauve petals with bright yellow anthers and is usually hard to find as it only opens in sunshine. Leaves straggly, green, long and narrow which help in locating where the flower might be growing. Found in sandy places, Pilcher Monument, Saut à Juan area and other cotil areas.

Autumn Squill, Adonis Headland

Asparagus Family – Asparagaceae

Autumn Squill

Scilla autumnalis

A short upright spike with blue-purple flowers clustered at the top. Basal, narrow, linear leaves appear after the flower. Mostly seen on cliff tops and in short dry grass from August. e.g. along from silver mines going west on Little Sark, Adonis headland and other coastal areas.

Asparagus Family – Asparagaceae

Bluebell

Hyacinthoides non-scripta

Dixcart wood, Harbour Hill and many other places are carpeted with these attractive azure-blue flowers in spring. The bell-shaped flowers with creamy anthers, loosely grouped near top of stem, droop when open along one side of it. Leaves long, narrow from the base. Some have now hybridised with Spanish Bluebell (*Hyacinthoides hispanica*) which is much more erect with paler blue flowers and blue anthers.

Spanish Bluebell

Bluebells and Thrift near La Coupée

Nettle Family – Urticaceae

Common Nettle

Urtica dioica

Very common, especially in nitrogen-rich soil, up to 2m tall. Mostly derided because of its stinging hairs on lanceolate, toothed leaves in opposite pairs on stem. But much liked by caterpillars of Peacock and Small Tortoiseshell butterflies. Tiny greenish flowers on long spikes at base of leaves. Separate male and female plants. Rich in iron and vitamins; makes a good soup!

Towards Port à la Jument

Spurge Family – Euphorbiaceae

There are two genera of the Spurge Family in Sark, Mercurialis and Euphorbia, with little in common except neither have petals, both are green, and have a milky fluid which is poisonous but has been used to burn off corns and warts which can be effective, I believe.

Euphorbia have flowers in clusters with one female and several male flowers, the clusters surrounded by an unusual cup-shaped structure called a cyathium (pl. cyathia), each with 4-5 glands on the edge of the cup, often horned. The cyathium is surrounded by bracts. Mercurialis do not have cyathia.

Sun Spurge

Euphorbia helioscopia

Annual with stems upright, hairless, solitary but branching near the top. Grows up to 50cm with yellowish/green flowerheads (cyathia) at first. Glands kidney-shaped, unhorned. Leaves roundish/oval and, unlike Portland and Petty Spurge, are toothed. Capsules smooth. Sometimes seen as a garden weed and in arable fields.

Spurge Family – Euphorbiaceae

Petty Spurge

Euphorbia peplus

A common annual euphorbia with oval to triangular-shaped bracts and kidney-shaped glands each with a pair of long, slender horns. Leaves oval, untoothed and hairless. Capsules ribbed. Found on roadsides, but also found near the sea and on cliff paths.

Portland Spurge

Euphorbia portlandica

A common perennial in Sark, seen mainly on cliff paths. Yellowish-green, triangular shaped bracts with kidney-shaped glands with a pair of horns. Leaves narrow, oval, untoothed, and pointed with prominent midrib underneath, alternatively up the often tinged red stem. Capsules warty.

Spurge Family – Euphorbiaceae

Annual Mercury

Mercurialis annua

Quite a common annual from the Spurge Family, one of two genera in Sark, the other being *Euphorbia*. Grows up to 50cm. Found on cultivated or waste ground. Upright, hairless, branched stems with greenish flowers, with no petals on long stalks. Leaves broad, lanceolate and serrated. First recorded in Sark in 1839 by Charles Babington.

Dog's Mercury – *Mercurialis perennis*, very common in England, but does not occur in Sark. Both plants have a milky fluid very poisonous to humans and animals.

Path towards La Jaspellerie

Cabbage Family – Brassicaceae

Lesser Swine-cress

Lepidium didymum

A low, pale green prostrate plant common on waste and disturbed ground with tiny, almost inconspicuous white flowers with 4 petals. Very divided pinnate leaves on a hairy stem. Pods smooth, notched, in two halves and stalked. Probably came originally from South America on ship's ballast. First recorded in Sark in 1896 by GT Derrick at Creux Tunnel. Only occasionally seen is Swine Cress (*Lepidium coronopus*), (not illustrated), which has larger flowers, less divided leaves, an almost hairless stem and a warty fruit with a beak. Considering its name there is no real evidence that pigs like to eat it, apparently.

Goosefoot Family – Amaranthaceae

Sea Beet

Beta vulgaris ssp. maritima

The dark green leathery-looking leaves are visible from early in the year along cliff paths. They look like small spinach leaves and can be cooked and eaten as a vegetable. Flowers sprawling to 80cm, tiny green, sometimes reddening, petalless, on long narrow spikes. Differs from *ssp. vulgaris*, Root Beet, in that the root is not swollen like the familiar beetroot.

Plantain Family – Plantaginaceae

There are four different types of plantain on Sark, Ribwort, Greater, Buck's-horn, and Sea Plantain. Their flowers are in spikes and leaves in basal rosettes.

Buck's-horn Plantain

Plantago coronopus

Short to 20cm, but usually smaller, the flower spikes brownish with yellow anthers, and leaves with little 'horns', like a stag's horn. Usually found near the sea from May to July.

Sea Plantain

Plantago maritima

A hairless plant, to 30cm, with greenish flowers on spikes, 2-6cm, with leaves thick and fleshy, sometimes slightly toothed with obscure veins underneath, and is found on bare ground near the sea from June to September.

Plantain Family – Plantaginaceae

Greater Plantain

Plantago major

A more robust plant to 40cm, with long flower stalks, usually hairless and broad, oval-shaped leaves with prominent veins beneath. Found on bare ground and in damp areas, from June to October.

Ribwort Plantain

Plantago lanceolata

Grows up to 50cm, often downy. Flowers brown on long spikes, with lanceolate leaves, slightly toothed and with 3-5 prominent veins on leaf. Found throughout Sark in grassy or waste ground from April to October.

Daisy Family – Asteraceae

Pineappleweed

Matricaria discoidea

The conical, pineapple-shaped disc-floret is yellowish-green, 5-10mm, single, encircled by green bracts with white tips but no ray-florets. Grows up to 35cm. Feathery green leaves alternate up the very divided stem. Introduced to England in 1871 from North America but originally from Asia and has spread rapidly. First recorded in Sark in 1923 by JR Le B Tomlin. Now common in fields, on roadsides and on rough tracks from May.

Carrot Family – Apiaceae

Alexanders

Smyrnium olusatrum

This is one of the earliest umbellifers which appears in Sark from April, sometimes earlier, with its green to yellow umbels (umbrella like structures) to 1.5m on stiff, hairless, grooved stems. Shiny dark green leaves with three toothed, oval-diamond shaped leaflets. It is said to be edible with the young stems cooked and eaten like asparagus, but it is a required taste. Originally a herb from Macedonia, the homeland of Alexander the Great, hence the name. It grows on roadsides and hedgebanks and is very plentiful.

Andrew and Shân Bache, Richard and Marie Axton on a botanical outing to Creux Belet

GLOSSARY

achene: a one seeded small dry fruit that doesn't split

annual: a plant that completes its life cycle within one growing season

anther: pollen bearing tip of the stamen

appressed: pressed closely or flattened e.g. hairs against a stem or leaf

biennial: a plant that takes two years to complete its life cycle

bract: a small leaf-like organ below the flower where flower stalk joins the stem

bracteole: when an inflorescence is branched the bracts on secondary branches are called bracteoles

bristle: a short, stiff hair

calyx: all the sepals of a flower when joined

capitulum: a flowerhead which consists of numerous small florets in the Daisy (Asteraceae) and Teasel (Dipsaceae) families, but which appears to be one single flower.

capsule: a dry fruit which splits to release its seeds

composite: member of the Daisy Family(Asteraceae)

corolla: petals collectively

crucifer: in the shape of a cross

cyathium (pl. **cyathia**): a cup-like structure resembling a flower in Euphorbias/ Spurges

disc-floret: one of the central tubular florets of a composite flowerhead, usually the Daisy family (Asteraceae)

downy: covered in soft hairs

filament: the narrow stalk part of the stamen which supports the anther

floret: a small flower which is part of a compound flowerhead or spike

fruit: seeds of a plant

gland: a sticky structure at the end of a hair or other surface of a plant which secretes a liquid

hip: fruit of the Rose family (Rosaceae)

inflorescense: flowering branches of a plant which include the stem, stalk, bracts and flowers

involucre: flower bracts which surround the base of the capitulum in Daisy Family (Asteraceae)

keel: in Pea Family (Fabaceae), the two fused lower petals, shaped like the keel of a boat

lanceolate: leaf shape, usually like a lance, the widest below the middle

ligulate: strap-like, the ray-florets in Daisy Family (Asteraceae)

linear: leaf shape, narrow and parallel sided

lobed: leaf and petal shapes, divided but not separated

midrib: central vein of a leaf

node: where the leaves join the stem

obtuse: blunt-tipped, usually a leaf

ovary: structure at the base of the pistil containing immature seeds

ovate: oval shaped

palmate: leaves that look like a hand with finger-like lobes

pappus: tufts of hair on fruit and achenes

pedicel: stalk of a flower

perennial: a plant that lives for more than two years

petiole: leaf stalk

petals: parts of the flower inside the sepals, usually brightly coloured

pinnate: leaf shape with leaf pairs opposite on the stem

pistil: female parts of a flower, consisting of the stigma, style and ovary

pod: seed case, usually long in Pea Family (Fabaceae)

pollen: tiny particles produced by the anther which contain the male gametes (sex cells)

prostrate: growing along the ground

phyllary: a sepal-like bract

receptable: in the Daisy Family (Asteraceae), the flattened part of the stem at the top which bears the bracts and florets

ray-florets: small strap-like flowers which form a ring around the disc-florets in the Daisy Family (Asteraceae)

runners: horizontal stems growing above ground which root at nodes and at the tip

scale: a small, papery outgrowth either brown or colourless

sepals: found below the petals in a ring, usually green

serrated: a jagged, saw-like edge

sessile: without a stalk, pedicel or petiole

sheath: found at the base of a leaf stalk and encircles the stem

spadix: a spike of florets in the Arum family (Araceae)

species: a group of organisms, in this case plants, which resemble each other

spathe: leaf-like structure in Arum Family (Araceae)

spike: an erect inflorescence, the individual flowers unstalked

spine: a sharply pointed projection e.g in the Rose family (Rosaceae)

spur: a slender tubular structure at the base of a flower, e.g. Common Toadflax (*Linaria vulgaris*) p. 38

stamen: male organ of a flower, comprising the anther bearing the pollen and a filament

standard: in the Pea Family (Fabaceae), the upper petal

stigma: the tip of the style where the pollen grains attach themselves

stipule: a leaf-like structure at the base of a leaf stalk

style: the part of the pistil, (female part of a flower), which supports the stigma

subspecies: a subdivision of a species which has differences in traits to the parent plant

tendril: part of a leaf or stem that is modified into a slender thread-like, sometimes twisting appendage, e.g. Common Vetch (*Vicia sativa*) p. 106

tepal: when petals and sepals cannot be distinguished from each other

trefoil/trifoliate: with three leaflets

tubular: long and cylindrical

umbel: a flower cluster with its stalks raised umbrella-like from the apex of the flower stalk e.g. Carrot Family (Apiaceae)

wart: a rounded growth on the surface of a plant

whorl: a group of leaves/flowers arising from the same point on the stem and encircling it

wing: the side or lateral petals on a flower from the Pea Family (Fabaceae)

Spring wild flower walk with Penny Prevel and Roger Veall

SARK BOTANY
(a brief outline)

Sark may be small, but it has held the interest of botanists for centuries. Since the first known written description of a plant on Sark, *Digitalis purpurea*, a Foxglove, but with white flowers, recorded by Thomas Knowlton on a visit in 1726, visitors have been fascinated by the variety of the plant life. On approaching the island by sea the sheer cliffs can appear rather forbidding, rising 300 feet above sea level, with hardly a hint of habitation. But Sark is full of surprises, with its plateau of cultivated fields and pasture, its heathland and wooded valleys, and a choice of roads and paths bordered by hedgerows which lead to exposed cliffs or rocky shores, all revealing varied and flourishing plant life.

Charles Cordale Babington spent five days on Sark, end July/early August in 1838 and noted 247 flowering plants and ferns which he recorded in his *Primitiae Florae Sarnicae*,* published in 1839.

This was followed by Dr Martin Bull who in 1872 published an article in the *Journal of Botany* Vol. X*, with additions in Vol.XIII in 1874*, in which he lists Sark plants, adding 89 new species to those already recorded by Babington.

Twenty years later Mr W F Miller from England spent two weeks in late August 1892 and added twenty six more plants to those already known. His findings were published in the *Journal of Botany* Vol. XXX* in November 1892.

The next contribution came from Mr G T Derrick of Guernsey who published three papers in the Transactions of the *Guernsey Society of Natural Science* Vol. III 1896*, 1897* & 1898*. In these he recorded 345 flowering plants and ferns, and included in brief notes on their locations based on his own observations. His papers included 50 which had not been noted before. He was surprised that there was not more affinity with plants from Jersey considering that the settlers in 1565 mostly came from there. One of the species which was abundant in Jersey, *Stellaria holostea*, (Greater Stitchwort) did not occur in Sark at all, but nearly a hundred years later it was sighted in 1988 by Mrs Marcia Marsden near the Collinette where it still persists today.

Mr E D Marquand wrote a section on Sark in his book *Flora of Guernsey and the Lesser Channel Islands*, 1901*. He mentions that Mr W

F Miller had handed him his complete catalogue of plants with localities for the less common species. As the earlier works of Babington and Bull did not include locations this, with Mr Derrick's records, was a very useful contribution. Besides the flowering plants which came to 410, Mr E D Marquand also lists 15 Ferns, 8 Mosses, 1 Hepatic, 89 Lichens, and 38 Seaweeds. Additions to the mosses under the title The Mosses and Hepaticae of Sark was published in *Transactions of the Guernsey Society of Natural Science* Vol. IV, 1903*.

Mrs Frances Le Sueur from Jersey and Mr David Mc Clintock undertook detailed work to record the most up to date list of Sark plants for *Atlas of the British Flora*, 1962. The result was published in *Reports and Transactions of La Société Guernesiaise* for 1962 under the title *A Checklist of Flowering Plants & Ferns Wild on Sark and its off Islets*, with a revised check list in 1979. Mr Mc Clintock also published *The Wild Flowers of Guernsey**1975, a book which includes records for Sark, with a Supplement in 1987*. He became BSBI (Botanical Society of the British Isles) recorder for Sark until 1995 when Dr Roger Veall took over and is our recorder to this day.

With the formation of La Société Serquaise in 1975 botany got a new lease of life under the supervision of Mrs Marcia Marsden. She was a founder member of La Société, its secretary for several years, and played an active role in botany, becoming the section head. With the card index given to her by Mrs F Le Sueur, compiled by K G Messanger from the Uppingham School Field Club of finds from their visits to Sark between 1954 and 1958, Mrs Marsden started a herbarium with the increasing number of specimens which had been collected since then. This was begun in 1980 and was the foundation of what is our **Sark Herbarium** today with 550 specimens (December 2009). In 1994 Mrs Marsden produced a *New Checklist of Flowering Plants and Ferns Wild on Sark and its off islets*. Her death in 2004 was a great loss to the island.

However, Dr Roger Veall had first met her in 1984, and he has been visiting the island at least twice a year ever since. Besides being BSBI recorder for Sark, he contributes much of his time perfecting the **kilometre square survey of plants** with his wife Psyche, searching for new plants or noting others less frequent, and keeping the herbarium up to date. Dr Veall also plays a major part in the **Wild Flower Fortnight** run by Tourism each year in late April/ early May, as an expert guide for specialist habitats. In 2001 he published *Plants of Sark*#, a very comprehensive and useful booklet which not only gives the location and who recorded it, from the earliest recordings by Babington 1839, but also indicates the scarcity value of a plant. He has also, with Mr Rod Stern, done research on bryophytes, and they have published their findings under the title *Bryophytes of Sark in Reports and Transactions of La Société Guernesiaise*, 2002*.

The Botany section endeavours to continue the good work of all these individuals both past and present and continually attracts regular visitors who take interest in certain aspects of the field. Dr Ann Allen and Dr Barbara Hilton have not only produced an interesting booklet entitled *Flowers of Sark,* 1993*#, a field companion with very useful drawings, while their extensive research on lichens resulted in the publication of *Lichens of Sark for Reports and Transactions of La Société Guernesiaise*, 1999*. They have also contributed to the study of Sark marine life, notably a pamphlet on *Invertebrates of the Rocky Shore*, 1989*#, and a pamphlet on the **Gouliot Caves***#, now republished as a booklet in time for the designation of the caves as a Ramsar site in April 2007.

Rob Waterman and Carolyn Heylar have been monitoring our trees for three decades, and have produced a wonderful collection of slides showing the changes over the years. Roger and Margaret Long from Jersey are among a number of expert botanists who visit each year and regularly contribute discoveries and rare sightings. We are greatly indebted to all who show such interest in Sark's natural environment and contribute to our plant records. Anyone wishing to see the herbarium should get in touch with Susan Synnott 01481-832314.

*Copies at La Société Sercquaise
Available for sale in the Gallery Stores

Near St Peter's Church

BIBLIOGRAPHY

Allen, Ann (1994) *Flowers of Sark, Field Companion*, Anne Allen & Barbara Hilton

Blamey, Majorie, Fitter, Richard & Fitter, Alastair (2003) *Wild Flowers of Britain and Ireland*, A & C Black Publishers Ltd, London

Blamey, Majorie, Grey-Wilson, Christopher (2003) *Wild Flowers of Britain & Northern Europe*, Cassell, London

Oxford Dictionary of Plant Sciences

Reader's Digest (2004) *Field Guide to the Wild Flowers of Britain*, Reader's Digest Association Ltd, London

Rose, Francis (1981) *The Wild Flower Key*, Frederick Warne Publishers Ltd, London

Spencer-Jones, Rae & Cuttle, Sarah (2009) *Wild Flowers of Britain & Ireland*, Kyle Cathie Ltd, London

Stace, Clive A, (2004) *Interactive Flora of the British Isles* (DVD-ROM), ETI (Expert Centre for Taxonomic Identification)

Stace, Clive A, (2010) *New Flora of the British Isles*, 3rd ed., Cambridge University Press

Sterry, Paul (2006) *Complete British Wild Flowers*, Harper Collins Publishers Ltd, London

Veall, Roger (2001) *Plants of Sark*, Roger Veall

Other books of interest for the Channel Islands

Bonnard, Brian (2007) *The Wild Flowers of Alderney*, Brian Bonnard, Alderney, Channel Islands

Le Sueur, Frances (1984) *Flora of Jersey*, Société Jersiaise, Channel Islands

Mc Clintock, David (1975) *Wild Flowers of Guernsey*, Collins, London

Ozanne, Bridget (2005) *Check List of Guernsey Plants*, Guernsey Biological Records Centre, Channel Islands

Silver mine, Little Sark

INDEX

216

Corn marigolds with Guernsey, Jethou and Herm in distance

NOTES

NOTES

NOTES

NOTES